REPRODUCING AUTONOMY

WORK, MONEY, CRISIS
AND CONTEMPORARY ART

BY KERSTIN STAKEMEIER
& MARINA VISHMIDT

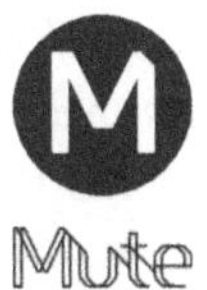

Mute

Publication version 1.1
GitHub commit SHA-1 ID 2644d6e –
2644d6e4aa3c4199a587071259d790543dd2e65

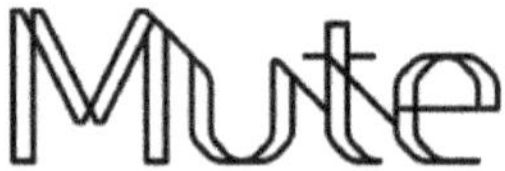

Mute Publishing - London | Berlin
http://metamute.org | @MuteMagazine | simon@metamute.org
Mute Books is an imprint of Mute Publishing
ISBN paperback: 978-1-906496-99-9
ISBN hardback: 978-1-906496-62-3
ISBN eBook: 978-1-906496-63-0

Free to download in a variety of digital formats and also available in print through pay channels
http://metamute.org/editorial/books/reproducing_autonomy
Distribution Anagram Books http://www.anagrambooks.com/
Editorial advisor English edition Anthony Iles
Publishing Management Simon Worthington
Layout and digital production Hybrid Publishing Group
https://hpg.io

Cover Image Johannes Paul Raether, *ResearchAvatara Species Transformellae 4.4.5.1: Insomation of The* Totipotential *CryoCommunisat*, Performance, Fridericianum Kassel, 25 June 2015, Photograph by Holger Jenss.

Acknowledgements

Thanks are due to Jenny Nachtigall, whose translation of the text into German for textem (Hamburg) proved a vital source of its sharpening and discussion in both languages and thank you to Johannes Paul Raether, who not only provided us with our cover image but also read and discussed earlier drafts of this volume. Thanks are also due to Danny Hayward and Anthony Iles for tireless, incisive proofreading and editorial dialogue, and to Halle für Kunst Lüneburg (Stefanie Kleefeld, Valérie Knoll and Hannes Loichinger) for commissioning the project and ongoing support, and to all who have hosted iterations of aspects of this work-in-process in public over the last few years.

The German-language edition will be published by Textem in 2017.
http://www.textem.de/index.php?id=verlag

CONTENTS

(NOT) MORE AUTONOMY

KERSTIN STAKEMEIER

1. The exclusive concentration of artistic talent in individuals and the suppression of it in the greater masses is the result of the division of labour.
   – Karl Marx and Friedrich Engels, *The German Ideology* (1846)

2. As no autonomy of art is conceivable without the concealing of labour, this becomes, within high capitalism, by means of the antagonisms growing from such dominance, problematic and programmatic [...] The artwork substantiates what ideology otherwise denies: labour desecrates.
   – Theodor W. Adorno, *In Search of Wagner* (1952)

3. What is theoretically right can be politically wrong. Theory is understanding and foresight, knowledge, that is, be it only one-sided, of the objective tendency and process. Politics on the contrary is the will to revolutionize this process, an all-encompassing rejection of its objectivity, subjective action, so that this objectivity cannot assert itself and does not carry off the victory. Theory is anticipation. Politics is intervening.
   – Mario Tronti, *Workers and Capital* (1962)

4. As visual art, a highly conceptual work still stands or falls by what it looks like, but the primary, rejective trends in their emphasis on singleness and autonomy have limited the amount of information given, and therefore the amount of formal analysis possible.
   – Lucy R. Lippard and John Chandler, *The Dematerialization of Art* (1967)

5. The work of art leaves the domain of representation to become 'experience', transcendental empiricism or science of the sensible.
   – Gilles Deleuze, *Difference and Repetition* (1968)

6. Efforts are made to avoid everything which could contribute to the articulation of this conflict between aspiration and reality [...] this articulation is avoided in a simple way [...] in that a certain part of life is severed from the societal one, is tabooed, in giving it the name private life [...] this tabooing entails that the specific exploitive relationship under which women are kept is suppressed.
   – Helke Sander, Action Council for the Liberation of Women speech at the SDS Conference (1968)

7. No theory can develop without eventually encountering a wall, and practice is necessary for piercing this wall [...] Representation no longer exists; there's only action – theoretical action and practical action which serve as relays and form networks.
   – Gilles Deleuze, 'Intellectuals and Power: A Discussion Between Michel Foucault and Gilles Deleuze' (1972)

8. The return to the immanence of the work in art [entails] the rigid separation of forming and acting [...] the end-result is the amputation of culture from its dimension of praxis [...] the obsessive fear of the artist without a work proves to be the heritage of the bourgeois fission of one and the same artistic process of production into art and life.
   – Peter Gorsen, *Transformierte Alltäglichkeit oder Transzendenz der Kunst* (1974)

9. A theory of socialization (is needed) [...] which understands Freudian 'individuation' as a working process and associates the artistic working process with it [...] early childhood socialization [is characterized by] the confrontation of the interfamiliar 'sphere of reproduction' with the later 'sphere of profession' [...] this separation of the sphere of production and that of reproduction relies on the identification of production-labour-profession, the sphere of production *posited* by society.
   – Gisela Dischner, *Sozialisationstheorie und materialistische Ästhetik* (1974)

10. One of the questions we have yet to answer is whether women do want the same things that men have wanted; whether 'greatness' in its present form is in fact desirable.
    – Lucy R. Lippard, 'Changing Since Changing' (1976)

11. What defines labor as such is not the production of a commodity or even a 'useful effect' [...] but rather the production of value that is appropriated by another as profit. What our modern myths of artistic production have effaced is [...] that the professional artist, like other laborers, works not only for his or her satisfaction, but for the enrichment of others.
    – Andrea Fraser, 'Creativity = Capital?' (1986)

12. The depicted [*dargestellte*] structure of capital is idealistic, its depiction [*Darstellung*] is not. Capital is depicted after the model of an absolute subject, the subject of theory in its dependency on the given

material proves to be a not-absolute, historical subject.

   – Frank Kuhne, *Begriff und Zitat bei Marx* (1995)

13. The submission of dependent labour can no longer be only formal, that means it can no longer take only the form of a separation of the labour force from its personalized bearer, but it must become real, the dependency of labour needs to be restored in its subjective character, in its singularity. It is the living labour as living, which needs to be subjugated.

   – Yann Moulier Boutang, preface to
Umherschweifende Produzenten (1998)

14. We frame the character's conceptual focal points. We might interpret a car commercial as a hairdo, an ideology as a designer skirt tone, a banking situation as a cheekbone, copyright issues as a jaw line, or maybe an application as facial agenda [...] It is the value of how things break down now.

   – Ryan Trecartin, 'Ryan Trecartin in Conversation with Cindy Sherman' (2011)

15. 'We called ourselves Chia Jen, or The Family', the choreographer Simone Forti wrote of the collective she lived in during the late 1960s. 'The life we lived in common provided a matrix for the profuse visions we lived out in various twilights' [...] Using Contemporary Art's self-reflexivity, it could be that anti-brands like American Apparel, achieving much of their psychic power from the real-time lives of their employees, are able to reach more deeply into the culture than art ever can.

   – Chris Kraus, *Where Art Belongs* (2011)

16. The usual effort to locate and identify the self, at once shifts into considerations about its deployment [...] The outcome is open, if one understands this deployment of oneself not only as competing for attention but as a critical gesture or revelation.
    – Karolin Meunier, *Return to Inquiry* (2012)

17. The phenomena of self-positioning, self-affection, self-referentiality as opening towards processuality, creation of possibilities, and initiation of becoming and mutation are originary. But these autopoietic spaces only gain materiality by transversalizing, repositioning and reconfiguring all realms considered as 'structural' (economic, political, social, linguistic, sexual, scientific, etc.)
    – Maurizio Lazzarato, lecture given at
    Psychopathologies of Cognitive Capitalism, Berlin
    (2013)

§

The history of art as that of the progress of its autonomy [...]
    – Theodor W. Adorno, *Aesthetic Theory* (1970)

And what is progress in art's autonomy? Simply *more* autonomy? But 'more' leans toward isolation as much as toward utopia, an uneasy ideal, a figure exceedingly unengaged and unrelated, unliveable. 'Less' does not sound much more promising, because heteronomy cannot principally be assumed to be only a loss of autonomy, but its commitments need to be justified in order to avoid becoming dependencies. Progress in autonomy cannot be – nor historically has it ever been – measured in quantitative units. Rather, the need for autonomy has been repositioned in relation to society's political, economic, and cultural developments on an ongoing basis. The collection of quotes that precede this text serve as a background to the brief and somewhat brutal historical grid I want to set up in order to locate notions of artistic autonomy and autonomies of art. These references not only offer an entrance into thinking about the role that autonomy has occupied in modern European intellectual history; they also put forward a thesis.

Autonomy in art is no longer modern and its modern forms, far from being the remnants of a lost ideal, are stabilising heteronomies whenever they are simply imported into our present. In modern times, autonomy was an abstraction from the reproduction of life, preconditioning the realm of art as one marked by a subjective excess of expression; in contemporary times, autonomy is a concretion, an individuation that designates specific figurations within this life. Its excess is one *of* life. I want to argue that autonomising strategies in the arts today are only significant where they actively counteract nostalgic modern notions of artistic autonomy.

I will construct a historical narration of autonomy's appearances in art from this perspective.[1]

Pre-histories

The quest for autonomy in the arts designates a social relation that developed historically with the distinction between manual and intellectual labour (see quote 1). Figures of artistic autonomisation can be traced back to the courtly arts of the late Middle Ages, where autonomy was pursued in the 'secularizing tendencies, which detached the forms from their genuine location and organized them after artistic principles addressed to visibility [...] in which the aesthetic meaning supersedes the symbolic and historical meaning'.[2] The development was later reflected in the social realisation of this proto-aesthetic formation: in order to not ideologically collide with the former religious or feudal use values of the artworks the artworks' early bourgeois acclamations had to render them purposeless, free from any applied function – ultimately *aesthetic*.[3]

The philosophical transfer of the political and juridical figure of autonomy as an ideal into the evolving realm of aesthetic practice makes an exemplary appearance in the writings of Immanuel Kant during the late 18th century. Out of his retrospective dictum that 'all philosophy is [...] autonomy'[4] rises the necessity that this intellectual conceptualisation of human self-determination bear an aesthetic side. This aesthetic side of Kant's conceptualisation of human self-determination was a capacity of judgement directed toward the outer appearances of the world that is destined to reflect them as one manifestation of the synthetic faculties of human reason. Kant introduces the 'heautonomy' of judgement,[5] a curious mixture between heteronomy and autonomy not yet directed toward art but toward the perception of its aesthetic 'primer': natural beauty. Kant systematically reintroduces autonomy at the core of all human potential, and heautonomy designates its sensible capacities. He identifies the philosophical realm of the aesthetic and forestalls art's modern claim to autonomy as a function of this realm.[6]

It remains important to underline the distinction of manual and intellectual labour as it begins to establish itself at the core of European intellectual history, before industrialised capitalism installed itself as the core of all human (re)production in the 19th century. One could argue that autonomisation came into existence as a social and artistic process of differentiation before autonomy came into existence as a socially and aesthetically distinct locus. It is this historical slippage that leads Theodor W. Adorno in the middle of the 20th century to attempt to sever the potentialities of autonomy from the capitalist implications it later became exposed to. Adorno employed the antecedent, more process-related understanding of autonomisation to loosen the capitalist determination of autonomy. Adorno wilfully constructed links through time between Kant's, Friedrich Wilhelm Joseph Schelling's, and Friedrich Schiller's pre-capitalist visions of autonomy and his own historical location in the 20th century in order to conceive an alternative fiction of autonomy that can sustain itself beyond capital and can be set against it. For this purpose, the philosophical disclosure of the historic distinction between manual and intellectual labour remains ineluctable – either in the form of Schelling's artist-genius or in Schiller's characterisation of an 'autonomy of the sensible'.7 But, as Adorno argues, artistic autonomy from life is the result of a heteronomous social differentiation of that life (see quote 2).

There were already strong theoretical objections to the affirmation of this differentiation by the end of the 18th century. The early writings of Karl Wilhelm Friedrich Schlegel, Dorothea von Schlegel, and Novalis established a concept of critique where the subject autonomised himself or herself not only by reflecting the object and thus distinguishing the subject from it, but equally by being reflected through this object itself, thus rendering their opposition obsolete and turning relations of representation into ones of mutual differentiation.[8] Schlegel polemicised against his contemporaries that 'views of totality, as they are in fashion today, are formed when someone overlooks all individualities and then subsumes'.[9] Kantian autonomy proved to be Schlegel's favourite example.

But the systematic fashion icon of such totality, Georg Wilhelm Friedrich Hegel, began to develop his philosophical system only a few years later. In his writings, however, 'autonomy' as a word hardly ever appears. It is used neither in *The Phenomenology of the Spirit* (1807), *The Science of Logic* (1812–16), nor in the *Lectures on Aesthetics* (1818–29). A reason for this absence is laid out in the *Elements of the Philosophy of Right* (1820), where Hegel criticises Kant: 'This "formal" is nothing other than interest, activity of the subjectivity in general. Autonomy is this (formal) self-determining'.[10] Autonomy, for Hegel, is nothing but a stepping-stone toward its own substantialisation as 'absolute spirit', which alone for Hegel is 'real'.[11] Autonomy necessarily remains incomplete, subjective, and relational, a quality which Hegel systematically strives to externalise.

It is in his *Capital: Critique of Political Economy* (1867) that Karl Marx systematically reintroduces autonomy, albeit under different premises. Marx does not employ it as a positive concept (or much at all), but it figures implicitly as a necessary undercurrent of his systematic contestation of capital's historical role as an actualised and industrialised absolute spirit [*Weltgeist*]. As Frank Kuhne points out, autonomy is the characteristic of capital's de facto dependency on the individual's engagement with it (see quote 12). Marx explains: 'the Hegelian dialectic [is] turned on its head, or, rather, from its position of standing on its head, it is placed upon its feet'.[12] The world spirit is hereby attacked by exposing its ultimately material and thus flawed synthesis. In understanding the emanation of capital's seemingly immaterial totality as a violent, historical, and material process, Marx enables a critical understanding of autonomy as a process no longer primarily intellectual but consisting instead of ongoing materialisations: processes of integration, functionalisation, separation, exclusion, and destruction.

Autonomy – A Capitalisation

In the phase in which historically the producers were cut off from the means of production the artist remained as the only one who had been bypassed – albeit by no means tracelessly – by the division of labour.

– Berthold Hinz, Zur Dialektik des bürgerlichen Autonomie-Begriffs (1972)

Within this general history of economic capitalisation, however, art's role has been a conflicted one, as Hinz, Marx, and Adorno have described (see above and quotes 1 and 2). Art's autonomy had been based on its conception as an intellectual faculty, and accordingly its value had been measured by its ability to represent the subjective capacities for intellectual consistency. Within the 'so-called primitive accumulation' (Marx) of labour in the 19th century – as Hinz describes above – artistic forms of production had remained relatively unaltered and came to represent an ideal of unalienated, autonomous work. Artistic forms of work had not yet been subjected to the division of labour.[13] Autonomy became art's economic and cultural emblem, its mark of distinction, and the core of its affirmative role within the social formation of bourgeois capitalism.[14]

The 'so-called primitive accumulation', as Marx argues, 'plays in Political Economy about the same part as original sin in theology'.[15] It constructs a foundational myth in which all history before capital turns into its pre-history so that lines of praxis become hardly traceable beyond capital's developmental scheme. Intellectual autonomisation herein is codified as intellectual property and segregated accordingly. The historical autonomisation of art was thus dramatically enhanced by the systematic capitalisation and industrialisation of life in the 18th and 19th centuries. Artistic production was subjected to so-called primitive accumulation[16] in that it was, as Marx calls it, 'formally subsumed under capital'.[17] Artistic production was severed from its ties to other applied cultural production and established as a discrete cultural, social, and economic realm in which the work expended bore no systematic relation to the value produced.[18] On the one hand, the industrial autonomy of art thus stood in contrast to capital's strictly reproductive measures: it served neither the reproduction of the labour force (not even that of the artist), nor did it produce a systematically measurable profit and thus an industrial average. On the other hand, it existed as an autonomous sphere only due to the division of all other labour. What had been instituted as art's supposed spiritual autonomy within capitalism, as its idealised subjective capacity, was deemed to be an exception, relegated to the margins. This was characterised by the ideological and material suspension of all social reproductive capacities and necessities, a structure already indicated in Marx and Engel's critique of art as a mechanism of social hierarchisation (see quote 1).[19] When Walter Benjamin wrote on artistic production and its mechanisation in 'The Work of Art in the Age of Mechanical Reproduction' around 1936, he spoke of expanding reproduction of autonomous works within modern capital, not of the reproduction of its workers – the artists. While the artwork is economically generalised, its producers remain isolated. Their 'negative' autonomy remains untouched at this point.

As a result, the autonomy of art was not an objective of the artistic avant-garde of the early 20th century; it was not regarded as the ineluctable precondition of artistic production. The autonomy of art was only retroactively systematically desired and instituted, namely after the second world war. Many Productivists, Constructivists, Realists, Dadaists, and Surrealists in Russia as well as in Europe were actively attempting to counteract the autonomy art had been afforded within bourgeois culture, to ruin the capitalist exemption-form art had come to acquire through its industrialisation. What Peter Bürger and others have discussed as the avant-garde's aim to overcome the division of art and life, an intrinsically artistic endeavour, was discussed in less compartmentalised terms by authors like Peter Gorsen as an ongoing attempt to regenerate art as an integrated social praxis (see quote 7). Most of the 'isms' listed above did not exist as discernible artistic styles at the time,[20] but were historically specific actions running through the field of art, which were later immobilised into spectacular, autonomous artistic schools.

One could argue that Adorno's postwar endeavour to recast the autonomy of art against the defeat of the avant-gardes in the first half of the 20th century within an 'aesthetic theory' attempts no less than to restage such an expandable understanding of artistic practices beyond styles, but acts from within a historical situation in which the field of intellectual labour, however contested, is the only one that remains open for such actions.[21] Adorno calls for intellectual labour against its capitalist compartmentalisation.

Autonomy – A State of Reproduction

At about the same time, another eminent figure of postwar Marxist theory, Mario Tronti, intervened against the segregation of life through its totalisation as a reproductive cycle of capital – though the direction of his approach was quite different to Adorno's (see quote 3). In Tronti's *Operaismo*,[22] autonomy appears as a position to be wrought from the disintegrated status of individual work as abstract labour. Where Adorno discerns intellectual labour as that realm of capitalist life that has not yet been fully subsumed under capital, Tronti presents autonomy as a necessarily tactical category of material labour. 'The autonomy of the political', he writes, 'proves to be a utopia, if considered as a directly capitalistic political project; it is the very last of bourgeois ideologies; it becomes sustainable, maybe, only as a labour claim'.[23] For Tronti, the autonomy of the political is a bourgeois operation obscuring the immanently economic nature of the political. Where Adorno locates autonomy in the realm of the aesthetic to construct a maximal distance from the reproductive brutalities of capital, Tronti argues that autonomy cannot be won at any distance from the production process but can be anticipated only as an autonomisation from within divided labour. Otherwise, autonomy within capital is, according to Tronti, nothing less than its driving force, because it is where labour 'appears to be an autonomous inner power of capital' that capital thrives.[24]

Tronti's reconstruction of autonomy as a category immanent to capital lays out the ground for an understanding of autonomy beyond its modern fate as a dialectically bound figure of emancipation and regression. As I intend to understand it here, he offers a reconstruction of autonomy as a figure of immanence and affirmation: not so much of capital as *against* it. Tronti's orientation toward the primacy of autonomisations in material praxis turns theoretical reflections upon autonomy upside down. Autonomy is once again brought into process. In analogy to Marx's understanding of capital as a negative *Weltgeist*, autonomy here fulfils the Hegelian argument against autonomy: it is systematically rendered as a merely formal, subjective, but necessary step within the fulfilment of the *Weltgeist* – that is, of capital. Thus, it returns as an affirmative figure of capital, but, as Tronti demonstrates, where this claim to autonomy is transposed into a category of a praxis against this actualised *Weltgeist*, it can develop self-affirming forms of material life that strive for the abolition of labour and capital alike.[25]

While Tronti focuses his discussion exclusively on the classical Marxist political subject, the worker, this transposition might also be – and was, in fact – refigured in other realms of capitalist life. The relocation of autonomy from a deficient developmental step of a subjective conclusion within capital to a transposed subjective emblem developed beyond and against it brings autonomy's aesthetic and political uses once again into closer proximity. Such an immanent understanding of autonomy repudiates the capitalistic distinction between art and life as an inadequate circumscription of subjective praxis from which nothing is to be won – and that under current conditions seems increasingly nostalgic (see quote 7). As Gilles Deleuze suggests, it denies the representative meaning of autonomy within bourgeois societies by strengthening its practical meaning; intervening into the relentless (re)production of capitalist totalities, it tries to traverse the institutionalisations of art and life alike. The subjectivism for which Hegel disregarded the figure of autonomy herein becomes its individuating potential.

This individuation has not least been attempted by feminist theoreticians like Silvia Federici and Mariarosa Dalla Costa, who, coming out of the *Operaismo* movement, demanded that autonomy be affirmed as a category of reproductive work. Their insistence on the productive character of the privatised, invisible, and – in Marx's sense – unproductive forms of reproductive work in the household enacted such a transposition: the transposition of a struggle for autonomy *into* a social realm deemed heteronomous. This is precisely what Helke Sander addressed in 1968 (see quote 6) when she declared that the political struggle for autonomy could not be achieved by displacing heteronomy into specific sectors of life.[26] Gisela Dischner's similar attack (see quote 9) on the social distinction of the 'sphere of reproduction' and the 'sphere of production' implicates art within this process.[27] She suggests understanding artistic processes as a potentially general factor of individuation, one that can enhance a more integrated conception of subjective development, counteracting not only the social exclusiveness of artistic actions (see quote 1) but also the insinuation of the distinction of production and reproduction into the process of subjective individuation.[28]

This social mobilisation of autonomy – its transposition from a perquisite of specific fields of intellectual labour to politics – provoked confrontations between persisting modern expectations, as Lucy R. Lippard and John Chandler characterise them in 1967 for the field of visual art (see quote 4), and contemporary practices, in which autonomy was no longer assumed as an ineluctable precondition of artistic work but the condition of *its* reproduction was brought into focus. In works by Mel Bochner, Lee Lozano, Adrian Piper, and others, the factual economic and social de-autonomisation of contemporary artistic practices became explicit. The understanding of autonomy on which their practices were based was no longer expressed in representative displays of subjective artistic fullness, but in purposeful autonomisations from modernistic (and utterly masculine) nostalgic stereotypes inside and outside of the actual *work*.

The advent of contemporary art through pop art and conceptual art socialised artistic production by actualising its economic status into a socially contemporaneous strand of cultural production.[29] Art was transfigured economically into a branch of mass culture. This development included the professionalisation of art education, the expansion and institutionalisation of art's distribution, and a strongly enhanced division of labour in professional artistic productions. The figure of formal quality was also actualised (see quote 4). It changed its meaning. Its Hegelian sense as a merely subjective and thus limited and particular fullness continued to be mobilised as a nostalgic modernist projection, but that same identification of formal quality enabled the mobilisation of autonomy as a dynamic figure *for* capital. What Yann Moulier Boutang describes for all labour in the 1990s (see quote 13) characterises the process of artistic labour's real subsumption, anticipated in the 1960s and 1970s: autonomy turned from an economically secured social locus of art into the social label of economically actualised artistic labour conditions.[30] And autonomy as an exclusive formal quality of art was counteracted by artists who began to recognise and strategically expose such formal qualities in everyday objects, actions, gestures, and deployments. What Moulier Boutang later characterises as life's subsumption under capital is transposed here. The subjective formalism of autonomy that Hegel indicated was capitalised and became a function of capital, which conceptual art disclosed in appearances of individuation beyond the subject.

Ten years after Tronti published *Workers and Capital*, Deleuze led a conversation with Michel Foucault entitled 'Intellectuals and Power', revisiting the question of theory and praxis (see quote 7).[31] And where Tronti had rejected the objectifying and thus ideological function of theory against praxis, Deleuze levels the two out. For Deleuze, the realm of art (see quote 5) and the realm of politics are distinct only as varying institutionalisations, different culmination points in 'a net of relations and transfers' in which the modern relation of representation registers as not much more than a brutal fiction, a stabilising social projection. Deleuze introduces a fundamental primacy of action, an autonomising move, but one that is no longer centred on the subject's intention and instead appears involuntarily, automatically. Representation is fundamentally rejected as a repetitive identification that systematically suppresses the differences that produce autonomising effects.

Autonomisation – A Praxis and a Standstill

In artistic production, practitioners like Andrea Fraser, John Knight, Alice Creischer, Andreas Siekmann, and others have based their praxis since the 1980s within the economic identification of contemporary art without subjecting it to representational escape strategies from capital. Fraser's argument (see quote 11) lays out the grounds of an integrated social artistic praxis that does not rest on the subjectivisms of its makers (for example, the projection of a genius) but on their systemic integration.[32] Arguably, this is the field in which autonomy operates artistically today, and one might even argue that it is this very same field into which the praxis of political autonomy has been transposed, too. This perspective *does* seek for strategies of de-capitalisation and anti-capitalist autonomisation, but it does not define those spheres of resistance in contrast to a more general sense of contemporary artistic and cultural practice. Rather, it seeks to lay open and expand internal systemic non-simultaneities, excesses, and breaches. Autonomisation herein might become a substantially affirmative process in which those moments of reality, of traces of a lived life, are cherished and extended as vantage points of possible autonomisations.

In closing I want to open up this enforced historiography of appearances of autonomy from within the rise, emancipation, and capitalisation of art by assembling a few recent motifs in art that concern such autonomisations within the present tense:

An historical understanding of form through art

In the productions of Bernadette Corporation, Isa Genzken, Josephine Pryde, and others, form – be it distinct formalisms or demonstrations of their breakdown – have become a medium to enhance the presence of the social materials of their art. Society's surfaces and objects, roles and statuses, turn into a naturalised pool of materials, a misguided arrangement on which artistic production preys without assuming bourgeois moral superiority (see Ryan Trecartin, quote 14). Form is employed as a weapon of real-time concretisation, of the autonomisation of forms of life against the real abstraction of contemporary crisis-ridden capitalist society. This is no longer a subject-centred autonomisation, rather one in which materialisms are not constructed but found.

An ongoing re-identification and re-individuation, via art

In opposition to the institutionalised spectacles of participation, an artistic self-deployment might act within an integrated field of contemporary art, but it recedes, bearing a developing repertoire of autonomisations, establishing a set of practices, of discernible gestures and discrete forms, that commands an arsenal open to collectivisations, quotes, and shared authorships, which can exceed the practices of art – as in the works of the late Ian White, Discoteca Flaming Star, Emma Hedditch, Johannes Paul Raether, Ulrike Müller, and others. (See also Chris Kraus and Karolin Meunier, quotes 15 and 16). Here, that subjectivity – which, within the modern idea of art, was idealised as an expressive genius – returns as a socialised component of its own productions. And it is in acting out this socialisation that autonomisations from it become legible.

A proposition of a non-functional, non-discursive, non-developmental singularisation within the procedures of art

In Maurizio Lazzarato's recent writings the global economic system of capitalism is portrayed within an ongoing process of violent disintegration. The expansive ideology of relentless economic progress has been historically locked down within a vicious cycle of debt, which Lazzarato characterises not only in economic terms but, notably, as the drama of a crisis of subjectivity. The capitalist crisis, in Lazzarato's view, has turned into a catastrophe and at its core lives 'the indebted man'.

In the 1970s, Lazzarato was part of the same Italian workerist movement of which Tronti had been a founding member. The collisions of this autonomist approach with the theories and practices of Félix Guattari have informed a simultaneously micrological and macrological understanding of autonomy, reconstructing possible modes of subjectivisation to overcome the historical deadlock of the present tense by way of a re-existentialisation of the subjective that is aesthetically as well as politically destined to struggle against the relentless endgame capitalism forces us into (see quote 17).

Referencing Félix Guattari, Lazzarato proposes a 'non-discursiveness', which in artworks like those by Monika Baer, James Richards, Amy Sillman, Susanne M. Winterling, and others, opens up affective points of concentration which do not expose a representative subjectivism. These artists do not appear as champions of the discourses into which they intervene, but as the cause of breaks within them. Crudeness, affects, desires, insecurities, and minor predicates are brought full circle instead of becoming part of a larger whole. Here, singularisations lose their developmental sense and spiral back into individuations; they do not strive for completion, but for expanding specification – autonomisations that want no functional, discursive place within contemporary catastrophic capitalism.

The modern ideal of the autonomy of the arts in all of the above-mentioned artistic practices appears as a representational leftover, which practices of autonomisation constantly struggle to overcome. The modernist figure of a somewhat prior autonomy of the arts fulfils a solemnly affirmative function within catastrophic financialised capitalism. It reiterates a nostalgic figure that can linger on only at the price of its social remoteness and conservative discursive function. Artistic strategies that have attempted to materialise instances of autonomisation, which have come into being with the rise of contemporary art in the 1960s, have, conversely, built lineages that span from art across society, across social strata and identifications. It is these autonomisations from within that map out ongoing trails of differentiation from capital, and that point toward a possible life without it.

Footnotes

1. I want to thank Danny Hayward. Without his anticipatory editing this text would have turned out significantly less intelligible.
2. Günter Bandmann, *Mittelalterliche Architektur als Bedeutungsträger*, Berlin: Mann, 1951, p.17. All quotations translated by the author unless otherwise noted [ed.].
3. A discussion of the genealogies of the aesthetic is found in Sven Lütticken's 'Autonomy after the Fact', where he argues that 'the aesthetic is a constant renegotiation of autonomy and heteronomy'. See Sven Lutticken, 'Autonomy after the Fact,' in *Autonomy: New Forms of Freedom and Independence in Art and Culture*, Jorinde Seijdel, Liesbeth Melis and Sven Lütticken (eds.), *Open*, no.23, 2012, pp.88–104.
4. Immanuel Kant, quoted in Joachim Ritter, Karlfried Gründer and Gottfried Gabriel (eds.), *Historisches Wörterbuch der Philosophie*, vol.1, Basel: Schwabe, 1971, p.708.
5. Immanuel Kant, *Über Phil. Überhaupt* (1794). This text later was published under the title 'Erste Einleitung in die Kritik der Urteilskraft', in Immanuel Kant, *Werke*, vol.5, *Kritik der Urteilskraft und Schriften zur Naturphilosohie*, Darmstadt: Wissenschaftliche Buchgesellschaft, 1983, pp.173–227.
6. The most consequential and materialist reading of Kant's writings in my opinion is still to be found in the writings of Peter Bulthaup. See, for example, Peter Bulthaup, *Das Gesetz der Befreiung. Und andere Texte*, Gesellschaftswissenschaftliches Institut Hannover (eds.), Lüneburg: Zu Klampen, 1998.
7. Friedrich Schiller, 'Kallias oder über die Schönheit: Schönheit als Heautonomie,' in Gerhard Fricke and Herbert

G. Göpfert (eds.), *Sämtliche Werke*, vol. 5, München: Hanser, 1962, p.400 and p.416.

8. For these writers, Karl Philipp Moritz and his novel *Anton Reiser* (1785) proved to be a major point of orientation, supported in opposition to the linear Enlightenment that Goethe's *Bildungsroman* of the time suggested. For an extensive discussion of Karl Philipp Moritz's *Autonomieästhetik*, see Karl Philipp Moritz, *Die Signatur des Schönen und andere Schriften zur Begründung der Autonomieästhetik*, Hamburg: Philo Fine Arts, 2009.

9. Friedrich Schlegel, *Kritische und theoretische Schriften*, Stuttgart: Reclam, 1978, p.84.

10. Georg Wilhelm Friedrich Hegel, *Werke*, vol. 7, *Grundlinien der Philosophie des Rechts*, Frankfurt am Main: Suhrkamp, 1986, p.381.

11. Georg Wilhelm Friedrich Hegel, *Werke*, vol. 3, *Phänomenologie des Geistes*, Frankfurt am Main: Suhrkamp 1986, p.729.

12. Karl Marx, afterword to *Das Kapital*, quoted in Louis Althusser, 'Contradiction and Overdetermination,' in *For Marx*, Ben Brewster (trans.), London: Pantheon, 1969, p.89.

13. The distinction between 'work' and 'labour' that I am importing here denotes the difference between what Hegel characterises in his early 'Jenaer Realphilosophie': '*Arbeit* selbst als solche ist nicht nur Tätigkeit, sondern in sich reflektierte, Hervor-/bringen, einseitige *Form* des *Inhalts*' (Work in itself is not only activity but is reflected in itself, creation, one side *form* of the *content*). See Georg Wilhelm Friedrich Hegel, 'Jenaer Realphilosophie', in *Frühe politische Systeme*, Gerhard Göhler (ed.), Frankfurt am Main: Ullstein, 1974, p.219; and what Karl Marx in 1857/58 distinguished as 'abstrakte Arbeit, die keine besondere Qualität besitzt und daher durch bloße Quantität meßbar ist' (Abstract labour, which carries no specific function and thus is measurable only by its sheer quantity); see Karl Marx, *Marx-Engels Werke*, vol.13, Berlin: Dietz, 1984, p.42. In the former, the individual uses tools to realise himself or herself in nature, while in the latter, the individual itself becomes the tool of the realisation of a value.

14. In *The Autonomy Project* (2011/12), a collaboration between the Van Abbemuseum (Eindhoven) and different art study programmes, initiated by Charles Esche and Sven Lütticken,

such distinctions between labour and work became equally central. See, for example, John Byrne, 'Use Value and the Contemporary Work of Art: Freeing Art from the Present Technocratic Framework', or Hito Steyerl, 'Art as Occupation: Claims for an Autonomy of Life', both in *Open*, no.23.

15. Karl Marx, *Das Kapital*, in *Marx-Engels Werke*, vol.23, Berlin: Dietz, 1984, p.741.

16. Danny Hayward made me aware of the fact that the 'so-called' of the original German text was initially dropped, and only later restored, in the translation into English. A momentous omission, as it eradicates Marx distancing from the ideology of 'primitive accumulation' and renders it as an affirmative category.

17. Karl Marx, *Das Kapital*, op. cit., p.531.

18. Steyerl, commenting on the passage mentioned in note 15, considers this as a 'refusal of the division of labour' on the part of art, which I find problematic in that the division of all other labour was indeed foundational for the autonomy of art and thus this allocation of agency presents us with a seemingly heroic but antisocial act.

19. See also Molly Nesbit, 'What Was an Author?,' *Yale French Studies*, no.73 (1987), pp.229–57.

20. An exemplary case of an art history beyond styles can be found in Justin Hoffman, *Destruktionskunst. Der Zerstörungsmythos in der Kunst der frühen sechziger Jahre*, Munich: Schreiber, 1992.

21. Juliane Rebentisch has made major contributions to the discussion around the contemporary relevance of a philosophical aesthetic and actualisations of autonomy in art. See, for example, Juliane Rebentisch, *Aesthetics of Installation Art*, Berlin/New York: Sternberg Press, 2012 (German version, 2003) and *Die Kunst der Freiheit*, Frankfurt am Main: Suhrkamp, 2012.

22. For an introduction to the history of autonomia, see Sylvère Lothringer and Christian Marazzi (eds.), *Autonomia: Post-Political Politics*, Los Angeles: semiotext(e), 1980; Steve Wright, *Storming Heaven: Composition and Struggle in Italian Autonomist Marxism*, London: Pluto Press, 2002.

23. Mario Tronti, quoted in Dario Gentili, 'The Autonomy of the Political in the Italian Tradition (Tronti, Negri, Cacciari)', in

Nathanial Boyd, Michele Filippini, and Luisa Lorenza Corna (eds.), *The Autonomy of the Political: Concept, Theory, Form*, Maastricht: Jan van Eyck Academie, 2012, p.13.

24. Mario Tronti, 'Fabrik und Gesellschaft [La fabbrica et la società]', *Quaderni Rossi*, no. 2, 1962, http://www.wildcat-www.de/dossiers/operaismus/qr2_tron.htm.

25. Ibid.

26. Speech by Helke Sander, 'Aktionsrat zur Befreiung der Frau', Frankfurt am Main, September 1968.

27. Gisela Dischner, 'Sozialisationstheorie und materialistische Ästhetik', in *Das Unvermögen der Realität. Beiträge zu einem anderen materialistischen Ästhetikum*, Chris Bezzel (ed.), Berlin: Wagenbach, 1974, p.99.

28. See Andrea Fraser's contribution to the *Autonomy Project*, suggesting that autonomy, understood in psychological terms, might be read as a 'defense function'. Andrea Fraser, 'Autonomy and Its Contradictions', in *Open*, no.23.

29. For a systematic differentiation of modern and contemporary art see Juliane Rebentisch, *Aesthetics of Installation*, Berlin: Sternberg Press, 2012.

30. Yann Moulier Boutang, foreword to *Umherschweifende Produzenten. Immaterielle Arbeit und Subversion*, Thomas Atzert (ed.), Berlin: ID Verlag, 1998, p.17.

31. Gilles Deleuze and Michel Foucault, 'Intellectuals and Power: A Discussion between Michel Foucault and Gilles Deleuze', in *Language, Counter-Memory, Practice: Selected Essays and Interviews*, Daniel F. Bouchard (ed.), Ithaca: Cornell University Press, 1977, pp.206-7.

32. Andrea Fraser, 'Creativity = Capital?', in *Museum Highlights: The Writings of Andrea Fraser*, Alexander Alberro (ed.), Cambridge MA.: MIT Press, 2005, p.32.

WHAT DO WE MEAN BY 'AUTONOMY' AND 'REPRODUCTION'?

MARINA VISHMIDT

What do we mean when we speak of 'autonomy' and 'reproduction' in the field of contemporary art? What kind of objects do these terms encompass, what are their histories, and what are their internal logical relations? And what can we say about how they operate in a philosophical discourse about art and within political theory and practice? In this text, I will analyse 'autonomy' and then 'reproduction', though in the understanding that this method of categorical isolation must be overcome if we are to reach towards the relationship of the two terms.

The Schema for Art

For a long time, I have been interested in how art is both like and unlike socially necessary abstract labour. Abstract labour is Marx's category for the social form of labour in a capitalist society. It is abstract because abstract value, represented by the exchange of money for labour, is what equalises all the different kinds of specific and concrete private labours. This equalisation is then what we call abstract socially necessary labour, and it sets the value of labour power and all other commodities insofar as they contain labour time, measured by this social average rather than in every specific case.[1] All labour in a capitalist society is thus at the same time concrete – insofar as there are specific kinds of labour performed by individuals in specific circumstances to fulfil a variety of needs and desires – and abstract – insofar as it is mediated by abstract value which applies across all of social production and which is expressed most purely in the form of money. This double character of labour reflects and is reflected by the double character of value in capital, namely use value, which is on the side of the concrete and particular, and exchange value, which is on the side of the abstract and universal.[2] Importantly, neither side can be separated from the other: our notion of use is coloured by our capacity for exchange ('do I really need this?'), and, whatever job we do, we better make sure it pays us enough to consume the use values we need (or want). This has important political consequences, affecting, among other things, the way in which politics is mediated in and by art.

According to the labour theory of value, art is not part of abstract socially necessary labour, because the activity of the producer in art is not determined by labour discipline, the quantity of the wage, nor by the productive investment of capital. Of course, an artwork may contain socially necessary abstract labour, whether it is the input of commercially available materials or the apparatus of mediation and production that includes everybody from administrators to installers to critics to cleaners. If art is seen as not just distinct from labour in capitalist modernity, but itself a product of the division of social labour, then it is evident that art also 'expels' labour as one of its conditions, on a systemic and on a conceptual level. This 'formal autonomy' from wage labour and capital is what renders artistic production both a material and an ideological exception to the capital relation, for modernist Marxist critics such as Theodor W. Adorno, and this exceptionality is called 'autonomy' – that which gives itself its own law, a definition established by Kant in relation to reason and also in relation to art, or rather, where art meets reason in aesthetic judgement. Art does, however, have a relationship to labour: like capital, it appears to be formally (or principally) free from labour, but is utterly dependent on it. Although both art and labour are subjugated by the social relations of capital, art's position in the relations of production makes it appear to be independent of social relations in a way no other kind of social activity can claim to be. The subordination of labour is ideally repeated in art: this is indispensable for the formal freedom, or *autonomy*, of art to take effect. Art must be seen as non-labour or transcendent in relation to labour, and this status was codified in what has yet to be fully dispelled – the Romantic-era concept of 'genius' – which was already in use by theorists of the aesthetic in the 18th century, including Kant himself. Yet both art and the subordination of labour are engendered by the division of social labour created to suit the needs of the real, not formal, freedom of capital. Art is thus subordinated to capital too, but under formally better conditions. It should be added here that this formal freedom was also often attributed a critical content, certainly in Marxist aesthetic theory such as Adorno's: a freedom whose roots were structural to capitalist social relations as much as to its own immanent laws. Art introduces a discrepancy into that which exists, thus posing a challenge to a world organised around work, accumulation, and power. Art is capable of displacing reality and disclosing its contingency.[3] Further, art, as a social activity without predetermined use or outcome in principle, is a source and site for the development of autonomy in the sense of free individuality. This would be evoking the universal individual that Marx posited both as the human being in communism and as a trajectory that bourgeois society has already begun to chart, in its perverse and limited way.[4] Ideologically speaking, and as Adorno noted, art is both a protest against the brutality of the world and a confirmation that this brutality has limits, preserving hope, akin to the role of religion: redemptive in its negation. This is what in critical theory was called the dialectics of negation and affirmation. More militant producers and theorists, though derided by e.g. Adorno as apostles of a problematic 'commitment', would over the decades and in specific conjunctures attempt to make this dialectic an immanently politicising force in art production.

The stand-off between art's 'negative' and 'affirmative' ideological role persisted from roughly the beginning of art's ideal and critical autonomy in modernity through the decades following World War II. Modernity here simply denotes the emergence of capitalism and the accompanying decay of feudal and religious matrices of support for artistic production. In modernity, art was situated as a circumscribed realm of freedom and purposeless creation in relation to the otherwise merciless 'natural' laws of property, exploitation, and expansion of economic and state rationality. For the most part, art was not industrialised and persisted according to artisanal and mystified relations of production, supported by private wealth, or by state cultural support in the 20th century. Art was supposed to take a sceptical or even hostile stance to both these phenomena (the power of money and the power of the state). Thus, art was sustained materially by the social arrangements it was supposed to negate ideally. As we saw above, Adorno called this problematic existence for art a dialectic between autonomy and heteronomy. In this framing, art's immanence to its own laws is a historical development which cannot simply be negated by fiat, certainly not from within art, as for example when art declares that there is no longer any boundary separating it from other aspects of capitalist social life, hoping thereby to overcome that life's strictures. Art was opposed to the world (autonomy), but it was also part of it (heteronomy). Consequently, it was always divided against itself: every expansion of art threatened art with its own disappearance, as the contours between art and the rest of the social world grew increasingly less distinct.[5]

However, according to conventional judgements, art is considered, since approximately the post-war period, to have entered its 'contemporary' period. This is not simply a convenient yet facile art historical periodisation. While the transition from 'modern' to 'contemporary' is undoubtedly a marketing issue as well as a taxonomic matter for historians and editors, the shift from one to the other has a further economic and theoretical resonance. We can initially identify a shift in the dynamic: modernity is a category in process (it is always related to 'modernising', a progressive temporal tendency), while the 'contemporary' implies a simple reification of the present (artistic contemporaneity inertly *coexists* with our present, or aligns itself with the times, is with our time).

The power of capital to subsume areas of social activity which are not directly value producing appears to have massively expanded in 'our' time and it has changed the conditions for art as an economic, as well as extra-economic, entity. This means that within the relations constituting the totality, there is a significant sense in which art has been displaced from the autonomy – relative or absolute – that was imputed to it in the modern period, or in the period of modern art. Art now enters much more directly into circuits of valorisation, be it in luxury manufacturing, brand enhancement, the 'experience economy', tourism, or gentrification. Its importance as an asset class has grown tremendously since inflated asset values, and the speculation in them, first became a significant basis for economic growth in the 1980s. It has also become much more visible in the disciplinary domain, with aspects of 'socially engaged practice' commonly included in the agendas of neoliberal social management, often in areas 'plagued' by disinvestment and 'diversity'.[6] If these developments reflect additional and more direct roles for art as a commodity or as social palliative, there is a further shift in the exclusive relations between art and labour, as object-critical and post-studio practices emulate various social services, whereas waged labour is encouraged to view itself as 'creative' in the most simplified and exploitative terms.

Under these conditions, the meaning of autonomy must also shift, as well as its relation to the heteronomy of extra-artistic reality as Adorno charted it in the recent past. In terms of labour, art has traditionally been the most individualised, opaque, and competitive of economic sectors, which is why it was the perfect prototype for labour markets defined by escalating precarity and 'human capital' investment strategies. Art has thus overseen an expansion of abstract labour fashioned in its own, albeit fetishised, image, even as its own production conditions have remained largely the same, which is to say, non-industrialised. This is not to downplay the counter-example of large and professionalised 'factories' operated by a handful of artist-entrepreneurs such as Damian Hirst, Takashi Murakami, or Olafur Eliasson, nor the global scope of the sale, exhibition, and discourse of art which has been established since the 1990s. These examples remain marginal, however, in the typical production conditions of art, which continue to unfold on a personalised and feudal basis structured by the artist-gallery-collector nexus and the opaque markets in which these actors move.

Nonetheless, despite all these contiguities and instrumentalisations, autonomy remains a presupposition for art, surviving close to a century of deconstruction and institutional critique. We don't need to demonstrate its survival on the level of discourse, because the survival of art itself as a distinct and highly invested form of social activity testifies to it. When we say that autonomy remains a presupposition for art, we mean autonomy as a style, as a marketing strategy, as a simple commodity niche. An easy example of this persistence of autonomy would be the distinction of art and design, which today is perpetuated by institutional and critical channels, whose own 'value' and legitimacy is derived from the contribution they make towards the reproduction of the distinction. Yet, in a certain fundamental sense, art can be conflated with autonomy *per se*, as its production is not bound by the determinations that constrict most other forms of social production in capital: art is endowed with the ability to suspend and displace all of these determinations *within its own sphere*. But then what happens to the critical or political content of artistic autonomy, to the autonomy of aesthetic judgement that Kant called 'purposeless purposiveness?'[7] To the status of art as a critical observation post, looking out on the rest of society, a sphere of 'research and development' generating dubious products with no immediate application? Unlike the marketing concept 'autonomy', this *critical* concept of autonomy is now in serious trouble. Like anything that has been held to exist in relative autonomy from the capital relation at one time or another, such as education, social welfare, or even labour itself, it has been affected, if not overtaken, by the effort of capital to expand throughout and progressively to subsume all of social life, in response to its ever more limited and short-term prospects for valorisation.

If we recall the earlier point that art, like capital, expels labour and declares a formal freedom from it while being just as subordinated to capital as any other form of social production (indeed, because art electively assumes capital's formal freedom as one of its own laws, we might argue that it is *more* subordinated), we can further say that this is possible because art is mimetic of capital in a very specific way: art mimetically assumes the role of the automatic subject of value. Thus, its subordination is not like the subordination of labour – it is not a form of subsumption – but rather an integration with markets, i.e. in the sphere of circulation and, when it comes to the production of subjectivity, of self-determining creative agency, in the sphere of ideology. This is the mimetic aspect which remains to be further determined.

Marx calls capital a 'subject' because it is self-positing, and also because it produces the (social, material) conditions which are at the same time its presuppositions. The world exists for capital, much as the world exists for the subject in Kant, insofar as the subject emerges in the transcendental synthesis in its relation to the world. It is likewise 'automatic', because it increases itself, realises itself as a condition of its continued existence without the intervention of any other agency extraneous to it: once a capitalist mode of production is established, capital survives by constantly positing the conditions it needs to reproduce and survive as the conditions for that society to reproduce and survive (wage-labour, property, and the commodity).[8] Kant's universality of aesthetic judgement finds its modern correlate in the universal capacity of creativity, which aligns the labouring subject with the automatic subject of capital. This is how art acts to socialise capital through images of creativity and flexibility which work in a wider context dedicated to abolishing the practical autonomy of labour via economic restructuring, legal constraints on organising, and the retrenchment of social insurance, mediated by the jargon of 'employability' and 'human capital. This turn highlights the only apparent compatibility between the two kinds of autonomy at stake: the autonomy of art (be it as artwork or institution), and the autonomy of the commodity, which constitutes *heteronomy* for the autonomy of art, or at least used to.[9] It is in this sense that we can talk about a growing proximity between contemporary art and abstract labour as social forms. Taking this into consideration, art's prospects for autonomy certainly seem to have dramatically shifted since Adorno's analysis was first published.

Now we are in a position to situate the beginning of the decay of the autonomy of art as a presupposition of artistic production to the autonomous subject of the artist herself. This decline in the autonomy of the artist is often connected to the debut of the readymade, which, as has been noted on many occasions, firmly established the sovereignty of the artistic subject over the contingent object of art.[10] The older universality of the 'genius' was thus joined to the irresistible tendency of nominalism ('anything which I call art is art'). The judgement 'this is art' thus migrated from an object to the subject, which ensured that the power – or the autonomy – of the art institution as the certifier of this art grew.[11] Thus, anything which appears in the field of art is art, and this remains the most solid institutional guarantee of artistic autonomy. But, as we have already seen, the critical potential of this development became etiolated a long time ago. The ability of art to 'accumulate' all social phenomena as instances of itself comes to resemble what capital does, in its self-expanding movement as the automatic subject. The nominalist gesture then appears symptomatic of art as a scene of, and vehicle for, the 'mimetic subsumption' of all non-value producing sectors. By this, I mean to say that art becomes a kind of production whose social power need only refer back to its own laws of motion (autonomy), rather than to any 'useful' or 'rational' economic basis of the kind adduced by economic reformists as the source and impetus of social development. In that case, the 'de-functionalizing'[12] of social reality and its circuits of use and exchange as performed by the readymade and its subsequent iterations comes up against a limit, that is, the limit that capital – trying to valorise itself in increasingly 'dysfunctional' ways in the current infinite 'downturn' – demonstrates to us on an hourly basis.

And at this point we arrive at the category of speculation, which casts the 'function' discussed hitherto in another light.

Elsewhere, I have referred to art as a primary example of the 'speculative' within the current phase of capitalism, and also to the relationship between artistic and financial speculation. To say that art is 'speculative' is at first glance to impute to it a form or method of thinking and doing which is open-ended in its relationship to means and ends and, thus, to (social) values and (economic) value. As already noted, anything which transpires in the field of art, even if it is identical in form to what transpires anywhere else, is very different in *function*: its function may alter or be erased altogether. This then is the phenomenology of art's autonomy, which itself can be shown to have evolved from a philosophical and political positing of autonomy as a state of properly human and historical creativity, invention of and control over the conditions of life, or, in Marx's terms, 'species-being'.[13] Speculation then seems to stand for the indeterminacy of autonomy, the openness to possible ends that belongs to a humanity finally taking on the law-giving maturity that Kant cited as autonomy's core feature. If we understand speculation in this sense, we can draw a provisional link between 'the speculative' and Marx's positive evaluation of idealism as a force for movement and change vis-à-vis the stagnation augured by the 'mechanical materialism' of 18th century Enlightenment thinkers.[14] The transcendental idealism of Kant is key here for Marx, though perhaps less so than the absolute idealism of Hegel, with its restless dialectical spiral. For Hegel, the speculative marks the place of autonomy for the human with regard to nature; it demonstrates the resistance of the subject to objectivity, giving her a principle of alterity within the totality. Autonomy is the point at which the subject thinks herself 'complete', before she encounters objectivity and realises that she is not, and that she has to universalise the reflection of the objective in the subjective in order to surpass autonomy and thus sublate individuality in the universal.

Proceeding or returning from here to a more structural analysis, we can situate speculation with relation to art by reference to the division between intellectual and manual labour, for which art acts as a sort of apotheosis. Why? Because it is in art that the division is sublated *as* mental labour: regardless of which task is done by the artist, it is not performed under compulsion and was an outcome of the inspiration that distinguished the artist from the artisan, although this inspiration is now professionalised in the ways that we associate with art practice today. Of course, the manual labour involved in artistic production is often outsourced, but the point is that, irrespective of who does what, the artwork is ultimately appropriated to the discrete identity of the artist. For Alfred Sohn-Rethel, all speculative thought, including, but not limited to, philosophy or art, is a product of the division between intellectual and manual labour. He traces this division to the emergence and predominance of abstract exchange (money) in the ancient world.[15] Abstract exchange separates what is produced from how and who produces it, and makes all labours equal, as we saw earlier with the description of abstract labour. Art then can be seen as one mediation of this abstraction, the abstraction which Sohn-Rethel describes as a 'social synthesis': the principle which organises how we live together in the form of a society premised on a collective experience of separation. We are literally connected *by* abstraction.

However, if art is the expulsion, rejection, or concealment of labour, it can also be the case that the recognition of art as itself a form of labour is where the speculative nature of art can take on a different guise. The performative disclosure of labour in art or art as labour may question the use value attached to labour while deploying a politics of labour as a negation of the conservative instincts attached to a norm of 'uselessness' in art. This may be done in order to confront a conservative notion of art as speculation with a more directly transformative one, which remains linked to the *social* character of art – which is to say, to the material practice of human labour – *in spite of its speculative character.* Speculation can turn into antagonism at times when the negativity of art in relation to use combines with the negativity of labour in relation to capital. The antagonistic possibilities or capacities of speculation viewed through the prism of labour, which cannot be cut away from its 'utopian' or undetermined side, further allows us to draw distinctions between the autonomy of art as status quo and the autonomy of the artist as a political entity in becoming. This touches once more on the 'de-functionalization' of the subject, that is, on the invention of the subject as a process immanent to art. Such a line of analysis begins to take us some distance from the modern concept of artistic autonomy, which in Adorno's terms was a 'windowless monad', reflecting its conditions but not itself acting on them.[16] Likewise, it may be helpful to retain and revise, rather than relinquish, other Adornian maxims such as that art is an 'absolute commodity', because it has no use value, only exchange value, and that this one-sidedness is one of the sources of its autonomy.[17] That precept could now be said to ground art's *speculative* power but not its autonomy, if we consider that commodities from luxury trinkets to structured financial products are also 'all exchange' without an atom of use value, and that contemporary art is just as socially useful as these luxury goods on a *systemic* level. A 'speculative power', on the other hand, is a power that issues from the contradictions that traverse contemporary art. Art still enjoys its autonomy of production, and for the same reason it maintains a high degree of critical energy; but this doesn't alter the fact that contemporary art is highly capitalised, or that it is constantly instrumentalised in the stylisation of capital accumulation worldwide.[18]

What now seems impossible to ignore is that art must directly confront the conditions of its own production as art in order to claim any kind of autonomy, *de facto* or *de jure*: an autonomy which then has to immediately open up onto the prospects for autonomous social activity in general. To do this, art has to confront its own character as an institution of reproduction – a service, an ambience, a deliberate dissolve between labour and signification – in order to ground its autonomy, that is, to once again stage that autonomy as problematic negativity in relation to capital. In other words, if the modern stakes for the autonomy of art had to do with severing itself from productive labour, conceivably to counter a world where mental and manual labour brutalised some and idealised others, the only hope for autonomy in contemporary art is for art to understand itself in relation to *reproductive labour*.

Why 'reproductive labour' rather than 'productive'? Reproduction is invisible, gendered, racialised, and biopolitically managed. It appears in art as an index of liberation movements in the 1970s, especially feminism. Production is visible and political; it echoes heroic Minimalism or early Soviet artist-engineers and artist-technocrats. Not all instances of production emulated within or transplanted into the field of art are as they seem. For example, Jens Haaning's *Middelburg Summer* (1996), which was a textile factory – with mainly Turkish workers – placed in an art centre and carrying out its normal operations therein, can be taken as an instance of the politics of reproduction in art, in the sense that art centres normally displace migrant-staffed textile factories in the process of urban gentrification; and also in the sense that the city is a contested territory in reproductive struggles, which can of course *also* take the form of wage struggles. In no small part due to feminist art historical scholarship and curating, the classic example of the incursion of reproduction into the field of art is now Mierle Laderman Ukeles and her early 1970s 'maintenance art', which involved moving the peripheral acts of institutional upkeep (cleaning, guarding) into the foreground as artistic performances themselves. In her 'Maintenance Art Manifesto' (1969), she questioned why the artistic practice she pursued in her studio and the housework she did at home should be kept so inviolably separate, and consequently, she questioned what regimes of domination and exclusion were propped up by the abjection of 'maintenance' and the concomitant elevation of 'art.' Ukeles thus sullied the sovereignty of the art institution – which by that point had come to ratify many artists, usually male, who identified their practice with industrial work or bureaucracy – with the banality of 'maintenance'. At the same time she sullied the autonomy of art with the heteronomy of domestic labour. Her gesture exemplified the political valence of revalorising reproduction as art: challenging the radicality of contemporary art by forcing it to look at its own conditions.

Thus, it is through the lens of reproduction that feminist art and curating in the 1970s, along with currents such as the Black and Chicano art movements in the US, the Art Workers Coalition, and others, forced art to recognise its relationship to labour, and to a politics of labour. Reproduction consequently revises the situation of autonomy, politicising the once merely 'critical' and mimetic relation of art to its others. We can also see a complicated and equivocal development of this tendency in the current era's interest in the educational and discursive in art, which, replaying '60s conceptualism in the era of financialisation, once again makes the process stand in for the object – and which thus, in a dematerialising gesture, switches critical attention towards the (pre-)conditions of artistic production.

Footnotes

1. See Karl Marx, *Capital: A Critique of Political Economy*, Volume 1, Ben Fowkes (trans.), London: Penguin, 1990, pp.128–29 and pp.138–39.
2. See Isaak Illich Rubin's discussion of abstract labour in *Essays on Marx's Theory of Value*, Miloš Samardžija and Fredy Perlman (trans.), New York: Black Rose Books, 1990, p.151.
3. This is the bedrock of all theories of art as a pedagogy in social change which rest on the concept of displacement of what seems natural and everyday. This can be seen in modernism from the 'making strange' (*ostranenie*) of Russian Formalism to Brecht's *Verfremdung* and as a broad strategy in contemporary art for much less defined critical ends, as in e.g. 'structural film' and all the practices that cluster around reflexivity as an ethic and device. The autonomy of art is here seen not as a presupposition but as a basis for praxis, as a means of exploiting the peculiarity of art's structural role in capitalist social relations as already something 'apart'.

4. In no small measure due to the alienating principle of exchange that is capable of dissolving ossified relations of e.g. personal or customary dependence.

5. 'Art and artworks are perishable, not simply because by their heteronomy they are dependent, but because right into the smallest detail of their autonomy, which sanctions the socially determined splitting off of spirit by the division of labour, they are not only art but something foreign and opposed to it. Admixed with art's own concept is the ferment of its own abolition'. Theodor W. Adorno, *Aesthetic Theory*, Robert Hullot-Kentor (trans.), London and New York: Continuum, 1997, p.4.

6. Though the debates on 'social practice' are extensive and cover a broad range of critical positions, some of the well known interlocutors include critics and curators such as Claire Bishop and Grant Kester. For a fairly recent examination of the relationship between art and urban redevelopment, particularly in the United Kingdom, see Josephine Berry Slater and Anthony Iles, *No Room to Move: Radical Art and the Regenerate City*, London: Mute, 2009.

7. The phrase is thus presented in the Pluhar translation of the *Critique of Judgment*, although the immediate context is not quite germane to a discussion of aesthetics – we are here in the section on 'teleological judgement'. See Immanuel Kant, *Critique Of Judgment*, Werner S. Pluhar (trans.), Indianapolis: Hackett, 1987, p.310.

8. In the first volume of *Capital*, Marx refers to capital as the 'automatic subject' in 'The General Formula for Capital': 'It is constantly changing from one form into the other, without becoming lost in this movement; it thus becomes transformed into an automatic subject. If we pin down the specific forms of appearance assumed in turn by self-valorizing value in the course of its life, we reach the following elucidation: capital is money, capital is commodities [...] For the movement in the course of which it adds surplus-value is its own movement, its valorization is therefore self-valorization [*Selbstverwertung*]. By virtue of being value, it has acquired the occult ability to add value to itself. It brings forth living offspring, or at least it lays golden eggs'. Karl Marx, *Capital: A Critique of Political Economy: Volume 1*, Ben Fowkes (trans.), London: Penguin, 1990, p.255.

Here we can understand that the notion of a frictionless self-production has resonant links also with a certain de-socialised but accepted notion of artistic genius, which functions *ex-nihilo* to turn indifferent material contents into artistic value.

9. We can say that a mark of the contemporary, since e.g. pop art, is that the heteronomy of the commodity becomes a site of critical value for an art exhausted with the enclosures of 'high culture'.

10. We can look at this from the standpoint of the relationship between art and abstract labour, as Claire Fontaine do in their 'Ready-Made Artist and Human Strike: A Few Clarifications': 'But we are not going to trace a genealogy of transformation in the domain of the production of art objects; what interests us here is what happened in the domain of the production of artists [...] In an era that has been qualified as post-Fordist, one in which on-demand has replaced stock, the only goods still produced on an assembly line – that of the education system – without knowing for whom, nor why, are workers, including artists'. Claire Fontaine, 'Ready-Made Artist and Human Strike: A few Clarifications', http://www.clairefontaine.ws/pdf/readymade_eng.pdf. Conversely, we can assess the 'readymade' as the marker of the art institution's 'primitive accumulation' of the whole of social reality, as does Andrea Fraser: 'The institutionalization of Duchamp's negation of artistic competence with the readymade transformed that negation into a supreme affirmation of the omnipotence of the artistic gaze and its limitless incorporative power. It opened the way for the artistic conceptualization – and commodification – of everything'. Andrea Fraser, 'From the Critique of Institutions to the Institution of Critique', *Artforum*, 44, no.1, September 2005, p.282.

11. Thierry de Duve, *Kant After Duchamp*, Cambridge, MA: MIT Press, 1998.

12. 'The status of art as a space for the de-functionalization of subjectivities: singularities emerge there emancipated from any utility. As a purely aesthetic space, the world of art harbors a potential critique of the general organization of

society, and of the organization of work in particular'. See Claire Fontaine, 'Ready-Made Artist…', op. cit.

13. The concept of species-being could be summarised by saying that the human is a species whose proper being is to invent itself. See Karl Marx, 'Economic and Philosophical Manuscripts', *Early Writings,* Rodney Livingstone and Gregor Benton (trans.), London: Penguin, 1992, pp.328, 386.

14. Karl Marx and Friedrich Engels, 'Theses on Feuerbach' in *The German Ideology,* New York: Prometheus, 1998. Thesis One reads: 'The chief defect of all previous materialism (that of Feuerbach included) is that things [*Gegenstand*] reality, sensuousness are conceived only in the form of the *object, or of contemplation,* but not as *sensuous human activity, practice,* not subjectively. Hence, in contradistinction to materialism, the *active* side was set forth abstractly by idealism – which, of course, does not know real, sensuous activity as such.' p.569.

15. Alfred Sohn-Rethel, *Intellectual and Manual Labour: A Critique of Epistemology,* Martin Sohn-Rethel (trans.), Atlantic Highlands, NJ: Humanities Press, 1978. This is a development which the recent film by artists Anja Kirschner and David Panos, *Ultimate Substance* (2012), seeks to evoke.

16. Theodor W. Adorno, *Aesthetic Theory,* Robert Hullot-Kentor (trans.), Bloomsbury Academic: London, 2013, p.6.

17. Ibid., p.31. It should also be stated here that I am deliberately abiding by Adorno's discussion of 'use value' to refer specifically to use value in a bourgeois capitalist sense, i.e., 'instrumentality', and not to the more developed and technical discussions of use value in Marx or other commentators. See also Stewart Martin, 'The Absolute Artwork Meets the Absolute Commodity', *Radical Philosophy* 146, pp.15–25.

18. This should not be read as a comment which applies exclusively to the 'laundering' operations performed on money when it is invested in the art market, but more broadly to the legitimating faculties imparted by the institution of art to less inspiring processes of value extraction such as real estate speculation. Having said that, as some writers have recently observed, the art market is not 'really' a market in the sense that it is extremely informal, unregulated and secretive: similar to the relation of art to 'the real', the art market highlights the fictionality of all

markets. See also Suhail Malik and Andrea Phillips, 'Tainted Love: Art's Ethos and Capitalization' in Maria Lind and Olav Velthuis (eds.), *Contemporary Art and Its Commercial Markets: A Report On Current Conditions and Future Scenarios*, Sternberg Press: Berlin, 2012, pp.209-240.

REPRODUCING AUTONOMY

KERSTIN STAKEMEIER
AND MARINA VISHMIDT

In the previous section of this book, we developed a critical genealogy of the concept of autonomy as it manifested in both the conceptual and the socio-economic conditions of art from the modern period up to the present. Central to this genealogy was an attempt to conceive of the significance of 'autonomy' for a materialist thinking, and in particular for recent developments in feminist theory and art. Now, in this second section, we intend to undertake a shared discussion of another aspect of the materiality of autonomy, this time by beginning with a category whose origins are found, not in aesthetics, but in materialist feminism and in the critique of political economy that it draws upon: 'reproduction'. Through a sequence of uncompleted and overlapping considerations, we propose to describe how reproduction as a historical category has changed through the development of modern capitalist social relations; to reject an affirmative and naturalising politics of the 'autonomy' of reproduction; and to establish the terms in which a more radical attempt to overcome the primacy of capitalist production might be conceived.

We begin, in other words, with a long set of difficult questions. What *is* 'reproduction'? How has it been conceived across the various traditions of Marxist theory and political aesthetics in the latter part of the 20th century up to the present? Is it only a form of 'preservational' labour, which, unlike production, is restricted to the *maintenance* of what already exists; and, if so, would it not have a *more* and not *less* distant relationship to political autonomy than the category of production? Can we continue to believe that reproduction under capitalism is primarily a problem for feminist politics, or has the concept now acquired new dimensions? And, once again, if it's possible to show that it has acquired such dimensions, what ramifications would this expansion of the domain of reproduction have for feminism itself, conceived in materialist terms as the practical rejection of the forms of gendered domination specific to contemporary capitalist societies - with gender abolition as its horizon?

Our inquiry weaves its way through six stages. In the first, we attempt to establish a new connection between 'autonomy' and 'reproduction' by pursuing an expanded conception of the former, freeing the category from the bourgeois ideology of merely *legal* self-determination, which is contingent upon bourgeois property relations, and relocating it in the technical matrices of contemporary human self-creation. We attempt, in other words, to establish an unfamiliar perspective on the relationship between capitalist relations of production and the 'self'of self-determination. We do this in order then to provide a new perspective on some earlier attempts to think 'autonomy' within the context of a materialist feminist politics. We approach these in the form of three 'critical models'. Critical model one offers a compressed assessment of the contribution of Italian autonomist feminism, and some related inquiries. Critical model two surveys the history of artistic 'de-materialisation' and its art-historical theorisations as a history of the concealment and exposure of reproductive labour. Finally, critical model three measures our expanded concept of reproduction against what we argue to be the repressive tendencies of a dominant concept of (reproductive) care. Thus we allow our discussion to unfold into a more speculative analysis of the works of some contemporary artists, whose practices, we propose, are so many optics into a more expansive, more concrete, and more energising theory of reproduction and autonomy than the ones we have lived with hitherto. The final section offers a summary and a conclusion.

Automatic Autonomies: Towards an 'Expanded' Reproduction

Who is the subject of autonomy? According to the dictates of liberal common sense, autonomy is a political concept referring to free individuals represented by their freely elected governments. From this perspective, slaves as subjects lacking in legal rights are heteronomous, while modern proletarians thrown into the industrial reserve army of labour and forced to eke out a life in the teeth of the workfare programmes of the modern state are autonomous. The autonomy of the worker is a consequence of his or her legal status as a free and equal subject party to non-binding wage labour contracts. The upshot of this peculiar definition is that autonomy is deprived of any meaningful relationship to what Marx called 'sensuous human practice', the most common form of which, in Marx's day as well as in ours, is patently *unfree*, compulsory, fragmented and physically and psychologically damaging labour.

Marx's critique of political economy attacked this practical ideology of bourgeois civil society by insisting that autonomy could only be materially conceived by restoring it to the context of human *productive* relationships. This was, no doubt, a great advance on much of the contemporary political theory of his era, not to mention what came after (cf. Hannah Arendt). But the autonomy thus reassigned to the productive worker in the form of a goal – the revolutionising of the material relations of production – leaves one assumption of bourgeois political ideology untouched, namely, the assumption that the sphere of 'reproduction' is one of direct domination, the sphere of nature which both communism and capitalism agreed was lost to history until it could be integrated with production.

Political objections to these assumptions were marginalised in modernity, although they became more visible with the New Left and de-colonial social movements of the past several decades. We can also look to recent philosophical work for the outlines of a theoretical counter-position, as well as to Marx's *Capital* itself.

In the last chapter we referred to Marx's idea of capital as the 'automatic subject' as the figure that unites the subject of value in capital with the artistic subject in a double idealism, and which expresses their shared reliance on a theology of self-creation *ex nihilo*, cutting labour – productive and reproductive – out of their circuits of self-expansion. In this section we intend to look at how this account of reproduction can be challenged by another one which draws on the politics of reproductive labour and its contestation of value and visibility in and beyond art, but which also sees radical possibilities in other approaches to abstraction focused on speculation, individuation, and performative indistinction.

The connections we seek out thus traverse different systems of thought in order to merge them through their relation to the notion of reproduction: the figure of the 'automatic subject', which Marx introduces in the passage 'The Transformation of Money into Capital', in *Capital* Volume I, characterises a disembodied reproduction that gives rise to an oblivious autonomy, relying on a merely self-referential, circular time. The automatic subject signifies the status of a dynamic of circulation, which systematically abstracts from the materialities of its cyclical movement in order to give priority to its perpetual re-initiation. Marxist feminists specifically, but, from the vantage-point of a 'pluralist empiricism'[1] also post-structuralists such as Gilles Deleuze, have insisted on the delusional character of a political analysis which simply repeats capital's vicious cycle, inside as well as outside of the subject, exactly where it attempts to develop a critique of it. Both have underlined the necessity of developing another language, another sociality and thus another set of categories to counter the ossified norms of identificatory critique. The objective here would be to envision an empirical understanding of autonomy as opposed to one arising as and from an abstraction. An autonomy *of* materialisations, instead of an autonomy *from* materialisations. An understanding of autonomy that seeks to undercut capitalist identifications with the individuations that traverse them. A denaturalisation of the subjects and objects of capitalism and an understanding of speculation that does not mimic the idealistic structure of capital, as it is characterised in the figure of value as automatic subject, but which emanates from an understanding that both alienation and autonomy are implicated in the relations of human life to the capitalist machinery which lies at the core of the reproduction of that life.

This is a trope that returns in writings by authors such as Lauren Berlant and Lee Edelman, in their understanding of 'affect' as a category that can undercut the fallacy of affirmative subjectivisation, of what they call today's fatal 'panoptimism'.[2] In response to this it seems crucial to also bring non-human apparatuses into the analysis, to acknowledge that the modern profile of autonomy does not extend to 'natural bodies' alone. Machinery within capitalism is not merely a tool, a means, but must, as Deleuze and Guattari discuss, be reflected in its being a material part of our present-day forms of existence, of our subject-being. Capitalist machinery is not external to our bodies, it is intrinsic to them. Thus a somewhat prosthetic understanding of technology and of the human body – an understanding that can surpass an idealistic perception of autonomy as a bourgeois token of 'the' modern subject – is in order.[3] As we want to underline with our concentration on reproduction, autonomy is a material and therefore also a technical relation. And even if the reproduction of capital and the reproduction of humankind may be non-identical, a simple reversal of our current modes of existence within alienated capitalist production cannot, and should not, be the starting point for a renewed conception of autonomy (this would only replace autonomy with some kind of primitivism).

Already in the 1950s Gilbert Simondon mapped out an understanding of the alienated existence of capitalist machinery *alongside* humankind, arguing that alienation within capitalism does not rest on the expropriation of means of production alone, but is also 'psychophysiological':[4] the technical objects of capitalism are tools that compel the human body's every move in exactly the same way, which have themselves been limited in the process of their development. This psychophysiological process renders technical objects and labouring subjects as alienated and incomplete means alike: psyche and physicality are indiscernible. While the expropriation that Marx referred to as 'so-called primitive accumulation' characterises an ongoing process, a (re)instating and expanding of capitalist property rule, Simondon senses a form of alienation that seeps into animate as much as inanimate matter through capitalist machinery. Since technical and human means alike are limited to their function *for* capital, and identified as property, their mutual limitation characterises another level of alienation. Only if this delimited relation can be challenged can reproduction be disidentified with formalised 'maintenance' and production with 'expansion' in such a way that both are de-hierarchised and autonomised from their capitalistically limited horizon of potentiality. Only if capitalist machinery is reconstructed to become prosthetic can reproduction turn into a re-construction of capitalist life at large. Autonomy, one might argue, thus depends on the purposeful expansion, reorganisation and individuation of heteronomies: those heteronomies that rule, form and reproduce our lives.

The practical and theoretical neglect of reproductive labour within capitalist dynamics, addressed, as we show in the next section, by Marxist feminists, continues to present the most significant and politically urgent starting point for a reconstruction of capital as a fundamentally material process. And Simondon's discussion of 'psychophysiological' alienation, as well as theories which, like those of Deleuze and Guattari, and more recently, Lauren Berlant and Lee Edelman, attempt to autonomise affects *within* rather than *from* alienation, complement the demand for an understanding of autonomisation that rises from a re-construction of the empirical terms of life under capitalism. Helmut Draxler has recently argued that the notion of the autonomy of the art work has to be understood as the modern subject's self-initiation – not an extra to it, which in this context seems very productive. If one follows Draxler, the disintegration of what Adorno discussed as the '*Werkcharakter*' (work character) of modern art, its appearance as a self-contained entity, and the distribution of autonomy are *in themselves* a work of affect, a psychophysiological process. Autonomy is, in Draxler's words, a category of the 'imaginary' at the centre of lived experience. It appears as an individuating process that is not primarily voluntaristic but which, quite on the contrary, constitutes a necessary social fiction.[5] We are arguing that the 'imaginary' of autonomy is materially inseparable from the individuated presuppositions of its reproduction.

The 1960s slogan 'The Personal is Political', for example, even today localises the social space of exclusion in the model of the nuclear family, the family wage and its foundational stigmatisations of women as encased in the 'personal', as well as the necessity for a personalisation of those terms of labour deemed 'public'. The politicisation of the personal and the personalisation of the professional go hand in hand. If we take this argumentation up once again, so as to take into account subsequent neoliberalisations of life and labour, it is clear that its analysis needs to be expanded and also modified. First of all, in times of economic crisis the biologisations of reproductive labour are nostalgically reasserted, but at the same time its motifs, actions and figures of socialisation have been distributed into vastly different segments of labour. Reproductive labour as a social location systematically opposed to productive labour has been economically identified and professionalised as low-paid 'service labour' on the one hand and has been identified as a mediating social 'skill' in all segments of the job market on the other. The pseudo-category of 'affective labour', introduced in Antonio Negri and Michael Hardt's recent writing, does not constitute a critical intervention, but rather naturalises a gendered capitalist adjustment of human affect as a contained and functional 'skill'. Their unabashedly positive, affirmative and feminised understanding of affect is effectively countered by Lee Edelman's insistence on affect as a potentially 'antisocial' political figure, a decidedly queer reconstruction of its conditioning, to which we will return later. And while industrial labour has (ideologically) been deemed to be vanishing – expanding the heteronomous character of its social existence even further – the technical objects which Simondon had located in those industries have spread, becoming instruments of our every productive and reproductive move. 'Productive' industrial labour and 'reproductive' housework, technical objects and human care have become interlaced as capitalist means. Affect itself is human as much as it is machinic. A renewed understanding of autonomisation can neither rest on an identification of the (industrial) worker-subject, nor on the (serviceable) careworker-subject. Furthermore, with the financialisation of global capital and its crisis, reproduction as a general term of human existence has become marked by anatagonism, so that while its localisation as feminine still unambiguously figures as its principal meaning, its social significance has expanded vastly and with it the autonomy to be spun from it.

As discussed in the first half of this book, besides reproductive labour, modern artistic production represented the second example of such an historically autonomised field of production within capital, another seemingly unproductive sphere of work, systematically detached and externalised *from within* capital. A social field which – in contrast to reproductive labour – mimicked capital in its dematerialising effects, at the same time appearing – in its gestures, in its avant-gardisms and exemplary forms of subjectivisation – as a counter-acting agency to capital's oblivious self-referentiality. Autonomous art and heteronomous reproductive labour were both socially identified, and economically disidentified, within the industrialisation of the 19th century. But 'non'-reproductive art and reproductive housework took on systematically opposed functions within modern capitalism. In the case of reproductive labour: extreme forms of both de-capitalisation (inherently privatised forms of labour) and capitalisation (providing 'pure' use value in the form of the production of labour power, the exchange value of which is severed from reproductive labour) (cf. Mariarosa Dalla Costa). In the case of art, extreme forms of both de-capitalisation (inherently privatised forms of labour) and capitalisation (providing 'pure' exchange value) are at work.

While art within modern capitalism appeared as the *mimesis* of capital, repeating its idealistic cycle of dematerialised self-perpetuation, of seemingly 'pure' exchange value, even as it demonstrated it in a field (seemingly) free of reproductive necessities, reproductive labour appeared as a devalued *mimicry* of capital, 'pure' use value, a repetition of its idealistic circle as a 'solely' material necessity, an enforced endless repetition. Mimesis, in the *Aesthetic Theory*, serves as Adorno's designation for an experience which transcends the subjective devastation of life under capitalism, enhancing a sense of subjectivity through the anticipation of art's autonomy, while mimicry is tellingly used in the *Dialectic of Enlightenment*, which Adorno co-authored with Max Horkheimer, to characterise a loss of subjectivity, a barbarisation of humankind into a state of first nature, the transition into an amorphous existence. Their juxtaposition seems as if it can be employed productively in characterising the roles assumed by art and reproduction as two kinds of exceptionalism to modern regimes of value, mirroring their social as well as economic stigmas.

The question here would be how, or whether, a reciprocal transference could be made to occur between the singularisation, individuation, expression, self-sufficiency and material exemplariness which were instituted as art's characteristics, and the projected finiteness, naturalised sociability and somatic, embodied and affective materiality instituted as the characteristics of reproductive labour. This move would project figures of autonomisation, which could suggest a new solidarity between those two poles of modern capitalist exemption. What could be the terms of a contemporary praxis which employs art's inherited modernist potencies but which begins with the critique of modernism's naturalised assumptions? Such a praxis would begin by viewing art through the optic of reproduction, as a question of artistic form and agency, of medium-specificities, of contemporaneity and of material autonomisations. So Draxler's correlation of artistic and subjective autonomy returns here, beyond the imaginary of autonomy, in a concentration on the embodied condition of autonomy. The 'politics of reproduction' can here stand as an optic that we can use to imagine degrees of transversality between the conditions for production and signification in art and the possibility of social struggles. The readings we develop of some contemporary and historical artistic practices later in the text will serve to flesh out these intuitions.

For us, such an inquiry implies the development not just of a newer critique, but of a concept of autonomy which both includes and exceeds its historical and political precursors. What is needed is a concept of autonomy that can make itself adequate to the current situation: a situation in which autonomy seems intuitively 'wrong' as an empirical or critical project in a world where 'subsumption' is the only terrain of action on offer. This would include, as we said previously, the strategic affirmation of the 'negative autonomy' of a sphere of production that acquires its critical purchase through its systematic isolation from social utility (the modern period of art), as well as the perforated autonomy of a contemporary art that is fully integrated with the speculative economic processes of financialised capital. An autonomy that is constructed out of the solidarity of art with its own terms of reproduction would not be a privative autonomy like the modernist one, finding its critical resources in its own special structure of production and affect and saving them for a better age. The autonomy at issue here would instead start out from its very integration to win for itself an autonomy with a general, socialised horizon. This is not to forget that this autonomy can only be achieved with the destruction of the system that denies autonomy to everyone who lives in it; the point is only that, as a result of its specific position, art does have its own resources for the articulation of means and suspension of ends. Such resources are capable of actualising dimensions of an as yet only glimpsed social autonomy, which can neither be subsumed into a general 'supecession and realisation' (as in the Situationist International),[6] nor treated as a form of inspirational social creativity based on self-evidently emancipatory premises. It remains distinct from that 'useful art' which accompanies and even, as in Tania Bruguera's conception, instigates social movements, but which in the end remains thoroughly dependent on its institutional-material premises and can only jettison its artistic framing as an artistic gesture. As we have shown, the question of autonomy for art is as problematic as it is constitutive. Adorno's description of art as the 'absolute commodity' is often, not incorrectly, taken to mean that it is absolute as an extreme instance of the triumph of exchange over use value, which obtains for all commodities. However, one implication of this description, which is less often discussed, is that it is also absolute because it is an extreme instance of the autonomy imparted to commodities by their fetishised conditions of production. Thus, autonomy and the fetish are not only indissociable, but it is art as a relatively distinct sector of social labour which embodies these fetishist relations most fully. And this is because of the autonomy that art's status within commodity relations paradoxically grants it: an exception from heteronomy as evident use value (though not the heteronomy of the market).

Critical Model I: Marxist Feminism

Marxist feminists such as Mariarosa Dalla Costa, Silvia Federici and Selma James took the consequential step of redefining unpaid domestic work as productive insofar as it produces the commodity labour power. This became the basis for the 1970s Wages for Housework campaign, whose not so secret aim was not an expansion of the social wage (welfare), to be administered by a benevolent state, but was rather 'wages against housework' – or the idea that if all activity was waged, exploitation would become impossible, and capitalism with it. This represented an expansion of the battle against value relations to the whole of social life. But, looking aside from the theoretical and strategic debates which persist on these questions, we can say that the pivotal aspect of this move, and the one that is still indispensable for any politics of reproduction, is that it severed the link between work and nature as a function of gender, reinventing the natural as social labour. Concomitantly, this can drive further our thinking about how the separation of art from use value can exceed art's traditional positioning of critical negativity to the existing and unfold on something more like a determinate, or emancipatory, level of negation.

It is perhaps generative here, then, to follow the premise of art's autonomy as grounded in its suspensive relation not only to 'use value' as a capitalist category but also to the concrete meanings of usefulness into another question. This is the question of how the negative relationship of contemporary art to the category of 'use' can help us reassess the seemingly self-evident usefulness of 'reproductive labour'. Firstly, we can ask in what ways art itself behaves as a form of social reproduction. If we remove the self-evidently useful aspects of social reproduction (i.e., as it is conventionally conceived: the maintenance of life) and see it purely as the work of reproducing society structurally, then we can see the systemically reproductive role art does play in the capitalist totality (T.W. Adorno), as well as the socially reproductive role it is called upon to play by state and capital, not to mention the 'socially practising' artists themselves.[7]

The problematic status of housework as reproductive activity par excellence, in that it seems not to produce anything, but only enables the production of discernible capitalist commodities to go on, can be addressed instead through its dimension of entropy and measurelessness. The entropic, limitless character of, e.g., housework starts to seem like a subjugated but basically functional analogue of the entropic, limitless 'activity' that in late 20th century art emerges as a sovereign form – a point already grasped several generations ago by 1970s feminist artists and their polemicists, such as Lucy Lippard. We can start to see how the social autonomisation of reproductive activity might be possible as soon as we cease to look upon it as *necessary*. As Claire Fontaine write in their 'Foreword' to *The Human Strike Has Already Begun & Other Writings*: 'The task of human strike is to defunctionalise all these useful activities and return them to their quintessential creativity that will unhinge any form of oppression'.[8] However idealist this notional jump cut might be, it contains a central question: that of undermining the 'use value' of all actions. This productively joins Claire Fontaine's 'human strike' with Edelman's 'antisocial thesis' as political strategies of non-compliance.

Having proposed that the systemic reproductive function of art in capital's totality today finds a shared negativity with reproductive labour, and that a common ground could be that both have a measureless and entropic character, a caveat is in order. Productive and reproductive labour cannot be so easily divided, at least not without considering the contested feminist legacy of that division,[9] as well as the extent to which aspects of reproduction pervade all labour, waged and unwaged, insofar as they reproduce both the worker materially and the capital relation structurally. However, this measureless and entropic character can only be read as common to both art and reproductive labour once reproductive labour enters the self-image of art. This is not to claim a privileged status for only the most liminal or networked or 'post-object' practices, neglecting their materialisation as spectacle or commodities, as in, e.g., the work of Marina Abramovic or Tino Sehgal, nor to deny the autonomising potential of practices which include objects among their modes of realisation. The point is rather that inasmuch as art and labour can be said to blur in their means and sites, it is in the work that is closest to the 'pure means' (Giorgio Agamben) of sociality as contingently value-producing labour that this porosity, and also the upholding of the polarity, can be most easily observed in its affirmative form. Here, what unfolds is not the entropic and measureless, but, on the contrary, the process of measurement itself.

In other words, we are not saying that art needs to be rendered immaterial in order to expand ties of solidarity with the reproductive structures inherent to it, rather that its genres and media need to radically transcend their seemingly 'pure' object appearance. Lee

Lozano's artistic conduct might serve as an example here: her radically deinstitutionalising practices within art, be that her *Drop-Out Piece* or her *General Strike Piece* (1969), or, for that matter, any of her documented social experiments which proceeded unmarked as 'pieces' apart from their documentation in her notebooks (e.g.: handing out money from a jar in a social gathering, not speaking to women) – were happening in an ongoing alliance with her painterly practice, in which she translated antagonistic stances into an antagonistic understanding of form, of material, of technique and representation. Lozano's painterly works are socially as radical as for example the *General Strike Piece.* This radicality is developed via media-specificity, as her paintings defy the conventions of minimalist abstraction as physically as her social experiments refuse the spectacularisation of performative practices. And even if such 'social' forms of artistic labour in most cases have resulted in the re-invention and continuation of such work as simply a service industry sub-genre of contemporary art, at another level, we can see these practices conjuncturally, that is, as art that no longer wants to be art, just as labour no longer wants to be labour (which, as yet, says nothing about the political determinations involved in each case). Lozano continued to exhibit while performing her *General Strike Piece*, as she attempted to play it out as a practice of *Gestaltung* (shaping) against art as a form of representative token, and the bleak finality that attends her gestures in retrospect was perhaps more nuanced, as the *Dropout Piece* (note the pun) shows. The instance of Lee Lozano, or of other women artists who 'dropped out' to do something else that didn't register in terms of their previous practice, such as German minimalist artist

Charlotte Posenenske, or who transformed those terms as part of embodied research inquiry into precisely the issue of individuation, such as Lygia Clark in her therapeutic practice, have a bearing on our discussion of reproduction as a category of solidarity within the field of art. This is because they represent a spectrum running from absolute negativity to negativity vis-à-vis art to an existential proposition which directly materialises social relations and subjectivity. The spectrum reflects the 'politics of reproduction' as a constellation of not always compatible but mutually generative moments, allowing for individuations and recompositions grounded in an immanent exclusion from art and capital as usual. In other words, Posenenske and Clark encountered the 'outside' to art from within their own work as artists, which prompted them to reject art's institutional role in its character as reproducer of bourgeois life in order to move instead through different reproductive mediations (such as therapy or social work) for their potential to organise social and subjective life differently. This bespoke a frustration with the *mimetic* character of art, which can only absorb other social practices as 'second appearances' (Jeff Wall) but cannot thereby forsake its legibility as art, which is both the source of its critical negativity and its acquiescence to the state of things. The position finds an echo in recent communisation theory such as that produced by Theorie Communiste or Endnotes, which often talks about a present in which labour no longer wants to be labour, and refuses to affirm itself politically as such, taking an interest only in those issues that relate directly to the conditions of its reproduction. For writers in the communisation current, this is incipiently revolutionary, since the affirmation of labour equates to the affirmation of value relations. However, another reading of the situation would see here a historical moment where the supremacy of capital is such that value relations dominate absolutely, so that even the weak negativity posed by the self-affirmation of labour finds no space. In any case, communisation theory does pose an important challenge to socialist nostalgias around labour – the nostalgias of a class belonging which seems to have lost the universality of its objective existence, at least in the West – as the motor of potential revolutions.

In these formulations, there is no possibility for the affirmation of labour in the capitalist present (nor, for that matter, of art) as a ground for critique, because the only critical possibility is fully inhabiting and 'weaponising' the constraint which each category, and the class-divided terms of their separation, place upon a re-orientation of collective revolutionary praxis in the present. The challenge to this scheme posed by reproductive labour, however, if we take it in the traditional sense of 'unproductive, gendered work', is that it has no positive content: its usefulness for reproducing society can be emptied. In emptying it, the moral valence of the 'hidden abode' of reproduction is rendered as inoperative as the sovereignty of publicly recognised waged labour (no less than the sovereign idleness of the art ideology) that it is meant to challenge. In this way, the axis of entropy and waste which connects reproductive labour to art can be fully conceptualised, building a relation of solidarity out of mutual negativity. This would be one first step in the 'weaponisation' of reproductive labour. If art continues to gloss social contradiction as its material, regardless of content or intention, than conversely art as a kind of 'human strike' ruptures this by performing the externalisation of those contradictions as waste and 'endgame'. If it succeeds, it is on its own terms and in its own language, but this language cannot be determined in advance: it has to be able to dramatise the potentiality of all living labour to persist as waste and negation in relation to the social whole. Labour, including reproductive labour, can act as a form of negativity in the space of art, helping to develop political possibility, as against the normativity of a creative individual subject faced with an objectivity which at best solicits complicity in the biopolitical grind of financialised austerity without end or block.

Critical Model II: Varieties of Obfuscation

By 'varieties of obfuscation' we signal our interest in creating a typology of the different ways in which labour gets concealed in plain sight in discourses around critical practice in art today – most often by the elision of the capitalist basis for the institutional divide between labour and art, an elision which means that labour can only reappear in art as a fetish, or as second nature, but never in its social banality and omnipresence, lest the social distinctiveness of art, and the critical capacities thereof, get lost in the process. A concomitant tendency that has developed out of the programmatic loss of distinction between art and other kinds of activity (even if institutionally the distinction remains intact until this day) is that labour that does not identify as labour sometimes becomes artistic practice. This is something we see demonstrated in the expansion and massification of educational and professional programmes in the field of art and curating. This is likewise a development that has been steadily accelerating since the 1960s, when linguistic and performative turns in art practice coincided with a purported 'dematerialisation' in the economy and, as we have shown in the two introductory essays, with the rise of 'contemporary', as distinct from modern, art.

What does this historical loss of distinction signify? If contemporary art has persisted through all its modes of critical and material interrogation in the past half-century, the obvious conclusion, and one which has been drawn many times, is that artistic practice can no longer be defined through its content, but must be understood instead through its status as a social fact (Adorno), its modes of experience (Rebentisch) or its institutional location (Danto). If anything can be done as art, then the act becomes supernumerary to the site or the grammar of its performance, and art becomes a term where non-specialisation and a 'laboratory' approach to activity is valorised and generates its own language and terms of identification. Some writers, e.g., John Roberts, but also Rosalind Krauss, have discussed this as a development that has augured a 'de-skilling' of the artist, but one which has been accompanied by a 're-skilling' in conceptual and social aptitudes that belong to other (in principle, all other) domains, such as the manager, the entrepreneur, ethnographer, curator, pedagogue, etc. The social content of contemporary art's autonomy can thus be seen as non-specialisation.[10] This non-specialisation seems to pose a weak form of negativity towards, or autonomy from, the narrow specialisation of humans as wage earners or privatised consumers, though some have queried the normative non-specialisation of the artist as a form of consumerism writ large (Andrea Fraser).[11]

Similarly, reproduction as a dynamic in art is a politicisation of art's own 'nature'. The natural ideology of modern and contemporary art is that it is a conceptual gesture whose substantive execution or material conditions are irrelevant, in accord with the proposal by Adorno and others, referred to above, that art 'conceals' labour like other commodities in capital, but that, due to its absence of use value, it does so to an even greater extent, and thus figures as the 'absolute commodity'. Now this bracketing extends to de-materialised practices, temporal processes and infrastructures, just as much as it once did to discrete artworks: we can now identify art's drive to render 'absolute commodities' out of these. A counter or a negative to such processes can be located in reproduction as a 'hidden abode' of de-materialised absolute commodities, and in particular in the way that they are thought about and presented. Concretely, this can mean outsourcing; gendered, racialised, migration-related invisibility of workers; or degraded working conditions as they stand in a determined non-relation to art-world academicism, i.e., ideal 'radicality', or criticality, without relation to its conditions of reproduction. Importantly, just as fair trade doesn't subvert production for value, knowing who is cleaning your Kunsthalle has no bearing on their working conditions. The cultivation of managerial virtue in the idiom of 'criticality' is perhaps the most disheartening example of this. Where non-specialisation is not a material criticism of the specialisation that is art, but just an activity which outsources labour or of the naturalistic exposure of its realities, its 'criticality' is an aesthetic, not a political, characteristic. Reproduction cannot remain formless within this account, just as art cannot remain formal: in their relation, artistic mimesis has to become an embodied process, and the mimicry of reproduction has to set out its speculative stakes. Both have to figure as states of one and the same negativity towards capital.

But we can also see the relationship between the institution of art and the politics of reproduction more broadly. The cell-form of art within neoliberal societies – though elements of this exist in the older or modern conception of the 'genius' as well – is the entrepreneurial artist who reproduces the institution of art in the act of reproducing herself as an artist. She is thus mimetic not least of the 'automatic subject' of value, which is self-reproducing as a social form once the necessary presuppositions (for capital: private property, wage labour; for art: the institution of art) are in place. Like the automatic subject of value, the artistic subject, when reproduced at the level of art as a social form, can only be reproduced by that which it absorbs and expels: labour. Consequently, like finance, the most familiar social instance of subjectified value since the crisis of 2008, everything that does not directly benefit art's reproductive circuit (whether in time or space) is turned into an indifferent externality, which then can yield further value by being re-absorbed as debt or rent in what has been described as the 'derivative logic' of contemporary art.[12] Likewise, art expels aspects of social life as waste – particularly those aspects which directly reproduce it – and re-absorbs them as material. As Marx has written, in relation to what he calls the 'tendential fall of the profit rate', capital is a 'moving contradiction' in that it strives to reduce labour-time to the minimum, while posing it as the measure of all wealth. The 'moving contradiction' has a double role in the field of art: it simultaneously flees and relies on labour (like capital); but the contradiction is also constantly at the risk of *becoming* labour, held in place by the ever infra-thinning edge of its autonomy. This means that, whatever political identifications are generated in the field of art, they can only ever be gestural or allegorical so long as they attempt to retain the platform art lends those articulations. This is especially the case with 'social practices' where it is only the professional imprimatur of art which provides the access to the material and human resources which allow it to register as such and not as, e.g., social work, i.e., *labour*.

Critical Model III: The Politics of Reproduction vs. the Legitimating Ideology of 'Care'

The putative disappearance of the distinction between art and life has thus become the central legitimating ideology of a bureaucratic and affirmative cultural practice. But what other utopian impulses have been appropriated by the theory-practice nexus of contemporary art? Now we turn to the relationship of the concepts of 'reproduction' and 'care'.

The premise we've been exploring so far is that the politics of reproduction as they transpire within the institution of art point to the emergence of a kind of collectivity. This collectivity would be defined by the recognition of contradictions; and also by the recognition of reproductive labour as the material condition of possibility for the institution of art and any autonomy to be found within it. This implies the shift from an understanding of medium-specificity, based on what Adorno in the *Aesthetic Theory* called the 'autonomous' genres of modern art, which he distinguished from the 'means-oriented' media of artistic production after 1945, to one of media-specificity, as Juliane Rebentisch has mapped it out in her 2003 book *The Aesthetics of Installation Art.*[13] In short, while Adorno understands what he calls 'genres' of art to be based on their medium specificity as purely aesthetic concepts, *media*-specificity positions artistic practices in relation to the reproductive valences of their media, and accounts for the fact that the notion of genuinely aesthetic genres of art can no longer be retained, when all artistic genres are shot through with the media of their (re)production, representation, distribution and exposition. Historically, genres in modern art were specified by their 'formal subsumption', their juridical identification as artistic means, for example whereby the painting of artworks and the painting of houses are systematically disidentified from each other. Media, on the other hand, are specified by their artistic appropriation, by the specific difference of their aesthetic usage and their industrial usage, e.g., the usage of epoxy resin as a sealing compound as opposed to its usage as a medium of painting. Accordingly, only the realisation of the coexistence of these media in art and reproduction alike leads to the potential volatilisation of the 'psychophysiological alienation' (Simondon) in labour, both in and beyond art. This simultaneous movement, then, has the chance of instigating a transversality between the weak autonomy of the artistic subject and those others, both within and outside of it, whose lack of autonomy is instrumental to the autonomy of the artistic subject. (This may of course have corrosive effects on both the self-evidence of the artistic subject as an artefact of institutional reproduction, and on the subjects outside that institution who identify with some kind of useful or productive labour.)

Reproductive and artistic labour thus share a potentially negative commons, a productively anti-social streak. This resides in the entropic and measureless, but also the preservative, somatic, sexual and psychological qualities of their serially singular appearances. As argued for already in the first two essays, artistic creation and reproductive labour alike turned into two model cases of neoliberal exploitation: affective and thus exploitative on an individuated level. However, the mimetic ideal, the constant conflation of (wage) labour and work as artistic achievement, seems ideologically much more attractive than its mimicry-driven counterpart, the contestation of both labour and work within the preservative, somatic, sexual and psychological qualities of reproductive forms of work. On the one hand we have the ideal of artistic mimesis, which presents an understanding of work as an activity which is measureless, or which can be measured only in terms of its merging of production and reproduction, of maintenance and creation, and which thus produces an over-arching subject. On the other hand we have mimicry-bound reproductive (wage) labour, in which both the maintenance and the creation are externalised as that of the system and not of the individual, and are thus separated by their systemic function. To this we might add that neither the nostalgia of work, which in art is bound to its modernist understanding as seemingly 'unalienated' activity, nor Michael Hardt's and others' more contemporary idealisation of 'affective labour' as de-alienating, can be said to represent much more than a regressive banality which resorts to gendered and classed naturalisations of categories arising out of early industrialisation. But for us – and for any theory that tries to show that work, rather than labour, could be identified as the core concept of a solidary collectivising form of human relations – the distinction of work and (wage) labour remains strategically productive in demonstrating that both care labour and artistic work, while remaining systematically distinct, are affirmative systemic functions. This could then be positioned against the legitimating ideology of 'care' as it is explored and inflated in contemporary art no less than in the aesthetics of contemporary activism. We seek instead the interconnection of care labour and artistic work via their potentially measureless and entropic qualities, via an understanding of affect as a potentially 'antisocial' force. Leo Bersani has argued in this direction already in *Homos* (1995): 'If there is anything "politically indispensable" in homosexuality, it is its "politically unacceptable" opposition to "modern bourgeois community"'.[14] In widening this argument beyond the 'Homo' by way of activating the notion of affect as a general phenomenon, Edelman, in his discussion with Berlant, proposes his 'antisocial thesis' as a queer rejection of the anticipatory mode: a rejection of what he calls 'reproductive futurism'.[15] It seems to us that rethinking this 'antisocial thesis' in relation to the social figure identified as the naturalised bearer of the future, the sphere of reproduction, helps to denaturalise its social bearings and questions its socially affirmative function. It is specifically because of its charged social identification that reproduction has the potential to act as a determinate negation.

This understanding of reproduction cannot be one that mirrors the naturalisation of human procreation. Gilbert Simondon's attempt to formulate an understanding of capitalist technicity as a series of sedimentations of human alienation within a material that needs to be dis-alienated in the process of human emancipation seems to offer a fundamental widening of perspective here. His identification of a 'range of indefiniteness' which he sees occurring as an element within the development processes of all capitalist machinery, but which is erased when this machinery is inserted into the processes of fragmented or subdivided labour, opens up a solidary perspective towards a possible re-purposing of the capitalist means of (re)production. Here, autonomy does not rest solemnly within the subject, but within the possible expansion of its 'body scheme' through a reconstructed understanding of machinery, a relocated 'range of indefiniteness', an embodied measurelessness in which the distinction of artistic (intellectual) work and reproductive (manual) labour can, potentially, wither away. In our sense, this might cancel the hierarchical distinction of reproductive and productive means of production, as what is technical and what is organic are no longer condemned to a relation of antagonism, but are repurposed, autonomised from their naturalised function for capital. The perforation of subject and object that Adorno offered (only) in aesthetic mimesis thus reappears transversed into an expanded sense of technical interaction: a mimetic (re)productive machine, in which autonomy returns as a relational individuation, a material border of abstraction.

By developing an expanded concept of 'reproduction' – or rather, since this is our principal claim, by reconstructing the expanded sense that reproduction acquires within contemporary capitalist social relations – we show that the reproductive politics of 'care' is at once a conservative naturalisation of historical forms of domination, *and* a misconception of reproduction itself. Moreover, however, we begin to move beyond a historically false opposition of 'reproduction' and 'production', or of dull maintenance and creative speculation. If the figure of maintenance is taken in our sense as an idiosyncratic and embodied *form* of speculation, then we see the rise of an understanding of autonomy that fundamentally counters capitalist subsumption: which spins forms of autonomisation from those entropic, measureless, somatic, sexual and psychological qualities which are peculiar to the capitalist ideologies of artistic and reproductive labour alike. In this account, the figures of maintenance and of art both share an antisocial inclination towards autonomy.

What does this mean for the 'politics' of art? Above all, it seems to us, one has to be aware of the gamble involved in advancing a politics of reproduction over a politics of production in the project of developing a more entropic and corrosive notion of autonomy for artistic production today. As production and reproduction are spheres which neither a job description nor the institution of wage labour can keep apart, and since both only make sense as stages in the reproduction of the total social capital, allying art with a politics of reproductive labour primarily makes sense because of the negativity of such labour in relation to the self-concept and social relations of art. In other words, while art has often been identified with and has recognised itself in the image of a liberated, world-creating labour, it recedes before the unglamorous and uncreative work of maintenance (unless of course this can be thematised as part of the aesthetic substance itself). As argued earlier, the labour politics of art often affirm its productive legitimacy in its striving for the regulatory institutions of contracts and wages, ignoring the development we traced above, where the purported solidity of wage labour – always gendered, racialised and very partial – is eroded by the tendency to render all labour 'feminised', that is, precarious, affectively dense and totally abstract at the same time. This shows us that reproduction is still part of capitalist value in process, such that the trajectory of autonomy that can be derived from it has to pass through manifest forms of negativity (or, as some current writers have chosen to call it, 'the abject').[16]

In proposing an artistic politics of reproduction in the expanded sense that we have attempted to set out, we should nevertheless be careful to underline the *ambivalence* of 'maintenance', insofar as its critical articulation within the institution of art can be seen as a ratification of that institution as the only site where capitalism's inequities can be alienated, staged, and then forgotten about again, insofar as the need of the institution itself to be 'maintained' is non-negotiable.

Readings: Reproduction in Practice

The time is ripe for a more sustained discussion of artistic projects that embody the politics of reproduction as a site – or, rather, a relation – of autonomy. Such a discussion has to encompass the significance such projects claimed at the time of their production, their historicisation in a corpus of critical and feminist practice, as well as accounting for the place they occupy in current feminist and art historical debates. One historical example we would like to evoke here is *Women and Work: A Document on the Division of Labour in Industry* (Margaret Harrison, Kay Hunt, Mary Kelly). A multi-component installation using photography, text and video footage to catalogue its 'results', this work confronts the 'aesthetic of administration' that established itself in the 1970s as a counter to a conventional mode of art making characterised by expression and affect with its own purist and academicising tendencies by means of its content: gendered industrial labour, the un-heroic conjunction of women and work. First shown at the South London Gallery in 1975, it comprises videos of routine work motions at a metal box factory, gridded presentations of photographs of workers containing data about their working days, comparative charts of male and female workers' daily schedules, and other bureaucratic accessories such as binders of documents. Here you can see how labour performs as the abject of art within art, even as art habitually abjects labour, especially women's labour, waged and unwaged. The affect of negativity, which is also the political anger of the work, derives from this. At the same time, the work showcases a tension between its immanent critique and the positivistic claims of sociology as an activist practice. Likewise, the tensions in 1970s feminist art over how 'women's work' was to be critically positioned – as an affirmation of the gendered abject (embroidery, biomorphic 'core imagery') or as an analytic exploration of systemic inequality – can be read here from a current perspective where gender appears in contemporary art as a commodified attribute to be mimetically affirmed or as an empirical status to be artistically elided, when not displaced into a diversity of political claims.

The feminist and materialist gesture here is to bring women's work into art as content through bureaucratic form, deploying means like statistics, time and motion studies, and factory reports not dissimilar to those incorporated into Marx's *Capital*. If the British conceptualist photographer Keith Arnatt noted several years earlier that 'The content of my work is the strategy employed to ensure there is no content other than the strategy', could this hold for a feminist and materialist art practice concerned to bring all the devices of conceptual emptying-out to bear in order to *make tangible* the factory, which, as Bertolt Brecht wrote some decades before, cannot be represented by the conscientious documentary act?[17] Other UK-based feminist activist artists of the same era, such as Jo Spence and the Hackney Flashers or the Photography Workshop, had a similar and specific relationship to the 'bureaucratic image' of that which cannot be seen in art – i.e., women's reproductive labour – and like *Women and Work*'s focus on women's low-wage and de-skilled industrial work, they deployed the same grid-like minimal admin-aesthetic of laminated posters, display boards and tabulations of statistics. The emptying-out of the aesthetic in *Women and Work* is here conducted through the agency of labour, albeit not in emulation of management or entrepreneurship, which is closer to the social position of the artist and was more common in the conceptual practices of the 1960s–80s. For materialist feminism, art is instead seen as another kind of mediation capable of actualising the abject as a material and political necessity. Thus, *Women and Work* constitutes an instance of the politics of reproduction in art, although its representational content is waged factory work.

A second early example of a politics of (reproductive and feminised) labour within art, albeit one which, to borrow Lucy Lippard's distinction, did tackle the 'action art' as opposed to the 'idea art' side of Conceptual Art, would be Mierle Laderman Ukeles series 'Maintenance Art' (which was already mentioned in the first half of this book). In 1969 Ukeles published the programmatic 'Maintenance Art Manifesto: Proposal for an Exhibition, "CARE"'. In it, Ukeles presents maintenance as the central characteristic of all life, and, more specifically, of art itself: 'Development systems are partial feedback systems with major room for change. Maintenance systems are direct feedback systems with little room for alteration'. Ukeles refers art and society to the elements that are usually blocked from visibility: its reproduction, its debris, its persistence and here, more specifically, its maintenance. Where Harrison, Hunt and Kelly in their *Women and Work* (1975) transposed the male gaze onto labour and through it demonstrated the absence of its female analogue, thus disintegrating its generality, Ukeles turns the normalised understanding of industrial waged labour around and envisages society through its reproduction, through the maintenance of its most basic functions. Through dealings with the abject, with dirt, and with decay, material transience becomes the core of all development. In line with the contemporaneous Wages for Housework campaign, Ukeles' manifesto opposes the social as much as the monetary value of these occupations: 'housewives = no pay'. She enacts a re-evaluation, which does not repeat the social naturalisation of reproductive labour but employs the field of art to enact and materialise an absent value form. In Ukeles' manifesto, two models are confronted: developmental and maintenance systems, which stand for change and repetition and which, though they may at first be opposed, will eventually be intertwined. These are historically positioned by Ukeles in the following way: 'Avantgarde art, which claims utter development, is infected by strains of maintenance ideas, maintenance activities, and maintenance materials. Conceptual & Process art, especially, claim pure development and change, yet employ almost purely maintenance processes'. Ukeles employs the idea of maintenance, which she, as part of her exhibition, practices – cleaning the exhibition space (e.g. 'floor paintings'), dusting off the vitrines ('dust paintings') and so forth – as her artistic labour, or, rather, as the grounds of all artistic labour and most specifically of that artistic labour which affects to have 'dematerialised' itself. The hierarchical conceptual distinction between a work and its execution is undercut along with the distribution of productive and reproductive labour and its gendering. Working with the museum's cleaners, Ukeles expands the social horizons of her critique of the gendered art/work divide to address the role of class and race. This is her artistic displacement of reproductive labour, a decontextualisation which renders such labour a negation of its social status and, at the same time, an affirmation of its position as the focal point of a change in perspective. Ukeles employs art as a starting point to undercut the division between productive and reproductive labour, and in allocating this contestation within a reinterpretation of avant-gardist and conceptual art practices, she finally questions the hierarchy and distinction of manual and intellectual labour altogether. In the work surrounding the 'Maintenance Art Manifesto', autonomy seems either to be consigned to oblivion or identified as a position within heteronomy. In line with Jean-François Lyotard's discussion of development as a 'metaphysics' propelling itself forward without any legitimating idea except its need for expansion[18] – like the automatic subject of value – maintenance can here be positioned as a singularising potential, to be acknowledged and also liberated from within the blind logic of development which masquerades as sovereignty and uniqueness.

The indexing of (re)production in art, as demonstrated in those two works, could be defined as gestural, albeit only within an expanded notion of the gesture which resonates beyond its historical moment and formal aesthetic means – a notion of gesture that is not a symbol but rather the signification of an expandable action. In both cases reproduction does not figure as the content of artistic labour but as one of its inevitable mechanisms. Thereby not only is reproduction opened up as a measureless space *in* art, but art is at the same time itself exposed to its inherent measurelessness. We are thus interested in the subjectivations, and also in the solidarity with the affective and material conditions of its (re)production, that art, through its own mechanisms, is capable of producing. Its 'own' mechanisms, the inclinations of artistic genres and media, act as a minimal and structural definition of autonomy, always in relation to the negation posed by its own role in systemic reproduction. This is a necessary, though far from sufficient, condition for a re-grounding of artistic autonomy as a political space, recognising that the taking of space (for action, for re-articulation) is the core political content of the concept of autonomy *per se*.

We should be clear that we do not want to encourage the current fashion of returning to the conceptual artistic practices of the 1960s and 70s as a kind of second-rate modernism, in which modernity and conceptual art are not discussed with respect to their contemporary status and actualities, but are instead merely imported from the past into the present as a privileged episode of politically accountable artistic practices. Neither *Women and Work* nor the 'Maintenance Art Manifesto' are contemporaneous to us, but, as mentioned previously, they are part of a moment in which Marxist feminists began to lay out the mis-location of reproductive labour within materialist and Marxist theory and organisation. Many of the phenomena confronted in both art and politics, then, have not vanished but have merely been updated: be it the feminisations of service labour, its naturalisation, the invisibilities of women in the industry or the unabated value identifications of artistic work as a life *sui generis*: as *new* life, unprecedented and obliviously autonomous from its own reproduction. The general terms of reproduction within the capitalist societies of the West have, as we pointed out before, fundamentally altered their proceedings, while at the same time remaining identical with themselves. So again, the terms of autonomy in the arts as well as in political organising, which were defined in the 1970s by feminist reconstructions of workerism as much as by female re-identifications of artistic media, did not become obsolete or simply outmoded, because what they contested vanished no more than did industrial labour, service labour, or the capital relation itself.

To put the same point more particularly: the industrial mechanisation which Simondon saw as the core of modern subjectivisation, its 'psychopathological' alienation, was not reconciled by the digitalisation through which the general terms of capitalist production have been re-aligned since the 1980s; rather, it was only actualised within its antagonisms. The same holds true for the unfulfilled utopia of avant-garde art as unalienated labour: it did not overcome the boundaries which separated its utopianism from the stark reality of the industrial (re)production surrounding it. Quite the contrary; this division was imported into contemporary art and prolonged there as a division within the modes of use to which its various media were subjected. This was, if you will, the capitalist fall from grace of conceptual art, in which exactly what signified the latter's drive toward the 'immaterialisation' of artistic media was used to introduce an industrial division of labour: a system in which the materialisations of art were executed by installation teams, production companies, gallery assistants or 'artist assistance'. (This, incidentally, is the structure that within contemporary art is often naturalised *as* art's autonomy.) So while the rise of the reproduction-oriented artistic practices of the late 1960s and early '70s seems to be easily decipherable and immanently political, it is perhaps less straightforward to identify exemplary practices of the politics of reproduction in art today.

Meanwhile there is an overriding concern with the 'reproductive institution', in the terms Louis Althusser developed in his 1970 text 'Ideology and Ideological

State Apparatuses'.[19] The school, the civil service, the workplace, the museum, and the psychiatric facility are approached as biopolitical apparatuses and narratives, whose conditions of possibility reveal broader social forces. This approach could be sketched on a continuum that links now canonic figures of institutional critique such as Andrea Fraser to those who have become visible in the past few years, such as Annette Krauss, Eva Kotátková, Pilvi Takala or Jill Magid. Their work is often processual, multi-modal, and performative in its execution. The difficulty of finding a position that convincingly fuses radical social critique with close attention to critique's political and institutional conditions of possibility can be demonstrated in the activist pairing of the fantastical with the documentary in the larger projects of Alice Creischer and Andreas Siekmann, which excavate the histories and ongoing parameters of coloniality – from Spanish primitive accumulation in 17th century Peru to Siekmann's isotype rendering of the 'conquest' of East Germany in the 1990s and Creischer's research-and-material-dense installations dwelling in and with modernity's production of subjectivity: a spectrum running from the conquistador to the tourist to the artist. We could also think of LaToya Ruby Frazier, whose documentation of the psychic (domestic) and recorded (industrial) scenes of economic and social decline in the small industrial city in Pennsylvania where she grew up proposes a new way to do realism, showing how the genre can be definitively seized and reinvented by one of its traditional objects – a black woman embedded in a 'problematic' context.[20]

These works contain speculation and reproduction in the way their social content is sedimented into their form. Sometimes this occurs by way of a speculative materiality, on other occasions via propositions for other social relations couched in performative modes. One instance of the latter could be a durational action, in which Frazier rubbed her Levi's-clad body along the pavement outside a Levi's flagship store until the denim was destroyed. The store – in a patent attempt to capitalise on the mythos of the post-industrial American city – had recently opened in her hometown. Others are the humans trapped in the small incisions in Eva Kotátková's elaborate tableaux. Kotátková's work emulates the precisely folded cartographies of those deemed to be insane. Human labour at once animates and is trapped in these mysterious worlds, which strangely evoke Marina Abramovic's living 'table ornaments', nubile young performers enlisted by Abramovic at a Los Angeles. art fundraising dinner several years ago, to much dismay.[21] Less contemporary, though coming to attention only in the past several years, is the work of Alina Szapocznikow, whose art compels through the versatile poverty of its materials, which are subjected to speculative metamorphosis, but with fidelity to the alluring and abject image of woman as the reproductive fetish of both art and market.

All these artistic endeavours were developed from critical revisitations of conceptual artistic practices and their after- effects and institutionalisations today, and they dispose of conceptual art's purity in favour of re-materialising and corporalising it. Creischer and Siekmann, for example, open up contexts of re-materialisation in which reproduction serves as a concrete point of orientation from which to redevelop history (as in the exhibition and publication, *The Potosi*

Principle,[22]) or contemporaneity (as in their recent shows entitled In the Stomach of the Predators).[23] Within an expanded, Althusserian sense of reproduction, one might argue that they seek to undermine culture's stabilising function for capital by specifying what reproduction *is* within the specific context of their work. Such strategies might not only appear within 'critical' artistic practices, which are already defined as political by their genre inscriptions, their belonging to the institutionalised field of 'political art'; they can just as easily arise from the so-called classical artistic genres like painting, sculpture or drawing, as in the case of Alina Szapocznikow. Already after the end of World War II, the boundaries between artistic genres and technical and mechanical media were perforated, generating an altered technical understanding of the nature of artistic production. Adorno already noted in his *Aesthetic Theory* that the distinction of 'autonomous' genres of art from 'means oriented' media was no longer unreservedly valid, because he registered the creation of 'autonomous' works from technical media, a glitch of autonomisation within the world of functionalism. The fulfilment of the modern utopian promise of 'autonomous' genres relied, on the one hand, on the fundamental non-simultaneity between art as a sphere of production remote from industrial technicality and all industrialised or industrialisable labour outside of it. On the other hand it relied on the understanding of this externalised technicality as an alienated and alienating monstrosity. In Juliane Rebentisch's writings the immanence of such a model is modified by what Rebentisch characterises as the state of 'intermediality' of contemporary art since the 1960s, a change which not only consists in the re-allocation of technical media *within* artistic genres – as Adorno had characterised it in relation to Dada in 'Art and the Arts' in 1967 – but more fundamentally in the recognition that the change from artistic genres to artistic media after World War II implied a fundamental impurity of those media, which manifested itself in the spheres of production, perception *and* distribution. Genre specificity had made possible the strict separation of artistic work from other labour, while at the same time technical media, and, more generally, extra-artistic sources and means, were incorporated into artistic production. But the media-specificity Adorno already witnessed in his time was still organised hierarchically from the genres of art – a fact Ukeles attests to when titling her actions as 'floor-paintings', 'dust-paintings', etc. – which functioned as headings under which to subsume and organise new media. From the late 1960s onwards this hierarchy faded, or rather was actively dispersed, leading to what Rebentisch characterises as an 'intermedial' media-specificity. This implies that the hierarchies of the media are adapted for art, a process that renders artworks utterly contemporary insofar as it is synchronous to developments in industrial reproduction taking place outside of art. Creischer and Siekmann's use of painting, sculpture and drawing as the core media of their artistic productions relies on and plays with this fundamental 'intermediality' of the most classical genres of 'autonomous' art, acknowledging their 'relative heteronomy'.

Adorno had recognised 'electronics' as a new medium from which artistic productions emanated in the 1960s, but this electronic paradigm itself underwent a fundamental reorganisation in its digitalisation in the 80s and 90s: the rise (and fall) of informational technicality. In the light of this development, intermediality itself has faced a crucial change. Today it might no longer be primarily the coexistence of different media within a work of art that characterises its intermediality, but rather the fact that all those different media are transmitted via a meta-medium that no longer distinguishes art from any other sphere of production: digitalisation. Within the crisis of financialised capitalism that began in 2008, what became apparent was that the spread of digital technologies throughout society, including their dominance in financial markets, occurred in such a way that they did not replace all antecedent media, as mechanisation had attempted, but reorganised the mode in which those media operated – their relation to one another, their timing, their matter. This is what we will discuss as the condition of digitality.

In this perspective the recent re-identification of digitality as yet another artistic medium – after its first new media boom in the 1980s and 90s – seems to be productive only where 'digital art' is understood as a shift within the roles of the medium, rather than as a celebration of its 'newness'. And if we look at the works of artists like James Richards, Jana Euler or Johannes Paul Raether, digitality, even though it is structurally situated at the core of their works, is not necessarily the mode of their presentation. Digitality instead becomes the lever to establish once again a somatic sense of technological matter, to expand a sense of timely machinic affect, and an expanded sense of reproduction, if you will. Richards' films, videos and slide projections all deal with historical states of image production and the cultural politics to which they are subjected. He remixes vastly differentiated sources, analogue as well as digital recordings, by means of digital video. Their now apparently general availability is set in motion by their digitalisation as a means to expose the materialities of their initial production. Richards composes affective lines of visual thought, constituting himself as the authority of the technical reproducibility of the imaginaries he digs into. He performs a de-differentiation of vastly differentiated historical forms of film and video: a practice of de-authorising, an appropriation by affective value only. Euler filters figurative painting through social codes, distributing the factors and pattern recognitions of contemporary digital social media. She thereby reallocates the genre she works in, the traditions, identifications and conventions it is based upon, within another, external but ultimately equally material horizon. As in Richards' work, reproduction is a perspective that emanates from entirely digitalised procedures which are materialised in the process of their artistic re-contextualisation. Reproduction is a technicity within the visual sources that becomes embodied in the works; it becomes a somatic, an affective quality. Richards' perspective is in no sense a productivist one, but one which recomposes production *from* representation. He does not approach his sources by putting into relation the capitalistic categorisations of the different forms of labour involved in their (re)production, but rather cuts labour out totally. Reproduction here is on the one hand a purely technical term, but on the other a deeply affective one. The reproduction of society and of individuation are strategically disconnected: affect alone determines the order.

Digitality is not immaterial, but it ideologically renders materiality as a second-order phenomenon. In the works we have just discussed, materiality is restored to the first order. This becomes even more evident in the performative works of Johannes Paul Raether. In his performances, theory, research, and documented information (both historical and contemporary) come together in fictional structures, in characters which embody the potentialities of their themes against their current realities: Protectorama, the world healing witch, tries to connect with her audience through their smartphones and mobile devices, and to employ these prosthetic devices as levers to remove capitalism's global spell; the Schwarmwesen strays across the urban metropolis, collecting tourist memorabilia in order to find its identity; and Transformella, Queen of the Debris, dressed in off-white latex, with a blond-braided wig and neon-pink skin, speaks to her audience about the apparently nonsensical existence of the nuclear family model within our times. She presents historical alternatives, such as Alexandra Kollontai's pedagogical theories, and current deviations, such as the industry around surrogate mothering on behalf of wealthy Western couples, and asks why humankind cannot be freed from such archaic hierarchies. Why has the nuclear family survived globalisation? Reality, and especially reproductive labour as it exists in today's societies, appears as an oddly alien construction, an ideological figure whose contact with the material possibilities of the present is irritatingly askew. In Raether's work, as in Euler's and Richards', the contemporary technicities of reproduction are what re-defines their capacity to present individuations by way of art. Autonomy is not a positive or pre-given attribute here, but instead something rooted in heteronomy. In the *tours de force* through history undertaken by

Transformella, the institutionalisation and naturalisation of the bourgeois ideal of the nuclear family is rendered absurd, and radically disconnected. Alternative models of procreation are merged in a narrative that autonomises itself not by offering a consistent alternative, but by rejecting this progressivist notion in favour of a 'pluralist empiricism'. Transformella speaks to her audience about the modern history of human procreation, its earlier socialist counter-models and its neoliberal professionalisations. The narrations are interwoven, they become inseparable and, far from pointing towards a utopian future, they radically question the social meaning of reproduction. If the nuclear family is rendered as a historical figure of adjustment alone, as the centre of a subject destined to be either reproductively functional or (more or less) pathological, human individuation becomes a rather transversal affair. In demonstrating the centrality and, at the same time, the irrationalities and brutalities of reproduction for the constitution of the modern individual, for what Draxler calls its 'imaginary', Raether brings about another imaginary: an imaginary that does not map a counterculture, nor a subculture, but that in its fictionalisation of documentary materials seems to insist that reproduction is always a fictionalisation, and one that can be autonomised from its social functionalism.

Conclusion: A Rather Transversal Affair

We have been arguing that the autonomy of art in capitalism is simply the peculiar form of its social integration, and that the tendency of this integration has been to provide, at worst, a justification and, at best, a mimesis of the 'creative autonomy' of capital from the social life that feeds it. The 'pathos of distance' (Nietzsche) integral to this version of autonomy meant that 'free' or autonomous art ended up glorifying capital just as surely as pre-modern art did the church or the nobility. Such an 'affirmative' role for art under bourgeois social relations, as was explored earlier in this text, meant that theorisations of the autonomy of the aesthetic, served, as often as not in spite of themselves, to harmonise subjective autonomy with the 'industrialised absolute spirit' of capital. Concretely, through distance and inversion, the spirit of capitalism and the spirit of modern art converged by adopting values such as contingency, idiosyncrasy, freedom, and the dissolution of established authority.

The subjective formalism of autonomy, which was already recognised by Hegel in the first half of the 19th century, subsequently became a function of capital, which conceptual art disclosed in the representation of individuation beyond the subject. Conceptual art – again, already in Marcel Duchamp – first became aware of art as a formal analogue to capital in its presentations. Eventually, this formalism and arbitrariness insinuated itself into its own productive and not just signifying processes. Abstract labour on a large scale suddenly became visible within art's characteristic methods- not just as an unmarked precondition for art, such as industrially produced art supplies. Conceptual art took the recognition of art as a formal analogue of capital to the forefront of artistic production. Delegation and large-scale fabrication as well as research enterprises became visible components equally of artists' market presence and autonomous works; a labour which was continually disavowed and occluded in the artistic commodity, in line with commodities in general. In other words, it is not just the art market, with its opacity and whimsical price movements, that comes to be a faithful microcosm of the structural logic of a financialised capitalism in which the notion of a 'real' economy can only ever be a nostalgic fiction. It is rather that such a capitalism enters not only at the level of exchange, but also at the level of the production of art and its institutions. It thus becomes aligned ever more closely with capital's central valorisation process: money making more money. And if financial commodities and artworks are produced and valued in similar ways, they also merge in a common image: the entrepreneurial, or artistic, subject as master of contingency and risk, a manager of the world as resource. Meanwhile, most subjects of devalorised labour are 'automated' as increasingly surplus 'human resources'; the contemporary twist on the old melancholy tale of reification which thought currents such as object-oriented ontology comically, if purposefully, misrecognise.

Subjectivity is encouraged so long as it aligns with that automatism, whether or not capital has any need for a particular subject or indeed for entire populations, both of which can be jettisoned wherever this proves to be necessary for the restoration of an acceptable rate of profit. As Pierre Hadot and Christian Laval have written recently, in a reflection on the iron law of self-enterprise: 'The novelty consists in triggering a "chain reaction" by producing "enterprising subjects" who in turn will reproduce, expand, and reinforce competitive relations between themselves. In accordance with the logic of the self-fulfilling prophecy, this requires them to adapt subjectively to ever harsher conditions which they have themselves created'.[24] This kind of nihilistic reflexivity – a self-aware but powerless mimicry of the conditions of capital's appreciation, treated as if they were the subject's own, even though they lead to the subject's disintegration and expulsion – often forms the possibility of subjectivity itself. The tendency has been discussed by Lauren Berlant as 'cruel optimism', and allows us to see how the promise of art as free subjectivation comes to take its place within and alongside the parameters of extraction and expulsion. We are here confronted by the fact that art can imitate with equal facility the obstinacy of reproductive work or the frictionless autonomy of capital, depending on the dominant logic of the era; and also by the fact that this is inevitable to the extent that art maintains its functional autonomy (or, rather, for so long as enough revenue can be diverted from capital valorisation elsewhere to ensure the equivocal survival of its institutions and markets).

The kind of differentiation and autonomisation experienced by art since the 19th century can now go no further, since all progressive tendencies on the part of the society to which it related – as a critical or sentimental reflexivity – have hit a wall. It would seem that any other kind of autonomisation for art would only be conceivable to the degree that such a process took root in the broader society, a form of negative transfiguration whose shape is yet to become clear. Such an autonomisation, depends, as we would argue, critically on the reconstruction of autonomy from an expanded understanding of reproduction. The potential measurelessness of both art and reproduction, their capability to bring the abject character of their own social existence into play, here might guide a way. It is not by merging into what exists that art can 'justify its existence', but only by envisioning and materialising the radical individuation, the estrangement, and the new solidarities required for a social autonomisation powerful enough to unlock the present.

Footnotes

1. Gilles Deleuze: quote in John Rajchman's introduction to Gilles Deleuze, *Pure Immanence: Essays on A Life*, Anne Boyman (trans.), New York & Cambridge MA.: Zone Books, 2005.
2. Lauren Berlant and Lee Edelman, *Sex, or the Unbearable*, Durham and London: Duke University Press, 2014.
3. This is something Paul B. Preciado has already begun to develop in his 'Manifiesto contrasexual'. Paul B. Preciado, then under the name Beatriz Preciado, *Kontrasexualles Manifiest*, Stephan Geene (trans.), Berlin: B_Books, 2002.
4. Gilbert Simondon, *On The Mode of Existence of Technical Objects*, Ninian Mellamphy (trans.), London, Ontario: University of Western Ontario, 1980. Available, dephasage.ocular-witness.com/pdf/SimondonGilbert.OnTheModeOfExistence.p
5. Helmut Draxler & Tanja Widmann, *Ein kritischer Modus? Die Form der Theorie und der Inhalt der Kunst*, Schlebrügge: Wien, 2013.
6. Tom McDonough, *Guy Debord and the Situationist International: Texts and Documents*, Cambridge, Mass.: MIT Press, 2002.
7. Such a precept of 'useless reproduction' sheds a new light on what political work the category of 'social reproduction' is being called upon to do in feminism and art politics alike.
8. Claire Fontaine, *Human Strike Has Already Begun & Other Writings*, London: Mute Books, 2013, p.8.
9. Endnotes, 'The Logic of Gender', *Endnotes*, no.3, 2014, pp.56-91.
10. Whether this also implies a de-signification of the relation of artistic practices to their media and genres is another question, albeit one which Rosalind Krauss and others have been answering affirmatively. Where a formalistic

understanding of 'high art' as an undisputed entity is held up, this de-signification really does apply – but where this affirmative understanding of art is disrupted, non-specialisation gains a medium-specific, a social content.

11. Here we would want to eschew the inference that non-specialisation constitutes a type of medium in some sense; the point is that this non-specialisation is at the core of many art education curricula today, and artists are socialised, in a certain bending of the stick against surviving conservatisms in the field, to assume that 'art in general' is simply the baseline condition of production for an artist today, that the artist is *de facto* a 'universal individual' even if *de jure* they are fully clued-in to critical models which would interrogate the axiom of 'universality'.

12. Melanie Gilligan, 'Notes on Finance, Art and the Unproductive Forces', *Texte zur Kunst*, no.69, March 2008, pp.146-153.

13. Juliane Rebentisch, *The Aesthetics of Installation Art*, Berlin: Sternberg Press, 2012 (German version Frankfurt: Suhrkamp, 2003).

14. Leo Bersani, *Homos*, Cambridge, Mass.: Harvard University Press, 1995, p.819.

15. Lauren Berlant and Lee Edelman, 2014, op. cit.

16. Endnotes, 2014, op. cit.

17. The debate on the representation in political film reached an apex in Britain in the 1970s in the journal *Screen*, with the controversy around *Nightcleaners* being exemplary of the mix of Brechtian, feminist and psychoanalytic concerns articulated there. See Claire Johnston and Paul Willemen, 'Brecht in Britain: The Independent Political Film (on *The Nightcleaners*)', *Screen* 16 (4), 1975, pp.101-118.

18. 'The striking thing about this metaphysics of development is that it needs no finality. Development is not attached to an Idea, like that of the emancipation of reason and of human freedoms. It is reproduced by accelerating and extending itself according to its internal dynamic alone.' Jean-François Lyotard, *The Inhuman*, Geoffrey Bennington and Rachel Bowlby (trans.), Cambridge: Polity Press, 1991, p.7; quoted in Devin Fore, 'The Time of Capital: Brecht's *Threepenny Novel*', 13 September 2013, http://nonsite.org/article/the-time-of-capital-brechts-threepenny-novel. Concise as this statement

undoubtedly is, it still acts as a provocative riposte to the postulates of 'accelerationism'.

19. Louis Althusser, *Lenin and Philosophy and Other Essays*, New York: Monthly Review Press, 1971.

20. A context which has all too often been fetishised from the perspective of race, gender or labour, or documented soberly in solidarity but from a well-marked distance, as noted in the critical writing and artistic work of Allan Sekula, Martha Rosler, et.al.

21. Documented, among other mass media coverage, by David Cohen, 'Who Will Rein Her In? Marina Abramovic versus Yvonne Rainer', 11 November 2011, http://www.artcritical.com/2011/11/12/abramovic-rainer/

22. Alice Creischer, Max Jorge Hinderer, Andreas Siekmann, (eds.),*The Potosí Principle: How Can We Sing the Song of the Lord in an Alien Land?*, Cologne: König, 2010.

23. Originally commissioned by the Biennale Regard Benin, Cotonou, the Bergen Assembly and the Istanbul Biennale in 2013. Also shown in different configurations in BAK, Utrecht, from 01.11 to 28.12.2014 and Galerie Barbara Weiss, Berlin, from 1.3 to 26.4. 2014.

24. Pierre Dardot and Christian Laval, 'The New Way of the World, Part I: Manufacturing the Neoliberal Subject', *e-flux journal*, no.51, January 2014.

www.ingramcontent.com/pod-product-compliance
Lightning Source LLC
Chambersburg PA
CBHW030117310326

42107CB00038B/574